My Hope Is Yours

A provocative exploration of the Creator's desire

Paul Ponticello

COMMON BOUND PRESS

Zionsville, Indiana

Common Bound Press
P.O. Box 146
Zionsville, IN 46077
www.mhiyours.com

First Printing, 2014
ISBN 978-0-692-02753-0

Acknowledgements
Adele Brinkley.........copyediting
Candice Crouch........cover photo
Joel Friedlander........design & strategy
Shelley Hitz............strategy
Caroline Ponticello....author photo

To Roger – *never down for the count*

The soul is dyed the color of its thoughts. Think only on those things that are in line with your principles and can bear the full light of day. The content of your character is your choice. Day by day, what you choose, what you think, and what you do is who you become. Your integrity is your destiny…it is the light that guides you.

—HERACLITUS, GREEK POET - PHILOSOPHER

CONTENTS

CHAPTER ONE

OVER THERE

Once again, it was the wee hours of the morning when I found myself awake, not fully conscience, but in a sufficient state of awareness to ponder my life. I picked up a local weekly newspaper from the floor and read of an upcoming concert by a musician described as a "free spirit."

Many years ago, I too had been pegged as one of these folks. Where had I gone? Then the dialogue begins. What are you doing "over here" if you were meant to be "over there"? Is there a way back? How did you fail so completely in navigating a life's journey that was so clearly laid out?

Living out what I was meant to be has not been so easy for me or I suspect for many of us. Reflecting on how I had managed to come to this emotional abyss is something I may never fully understand. Living the "free spirit" life had led to one filled with constraints and much despair. Those considered spiritual masters indicate that we eventually learn to live with our own contradictions. My ability to discern this nugget of wisdom has given me a glimmer of that proverbial "hope" in humble new beginnings.

On a cold wintry afternoon a few years back, I wondered into a book store in Traverse City, Michigan. I was passing time as I thought about the significance of the twists and turns that led me to be in that part of the country. Although I didn't know it then, forces greater than my own conspired to begin a mid course correction in my life's direction.

Rather than peruse the usual sections, I chose to meander through the spiritual stacks where I found books by folks peddling all sorts of solutions for the spiritual ailments of our times like the real estate guru's hawking rags to riches just a few aisles over. Sell, sell, and sell. The searching mind represents a glaring opportunity to be exploited by captivating and hopeful marketing. At least, I did not spot any "Idiots" guide to spiritual well being. I am not an idiot. Are you? Nor did I find self help guides to death and dying. I am weary of self-help. It may be useful when it comes to vending machines but leaves much to be desired in cultivating nurturing human relationships. My skepticism abated sufficiently long enough to find in others' journeys the seeds to rekindle my own.

Thus far, I have learned to send less energy to what I have done and what I have failed to do to what I was meant to do and be. The middle of the night jaunts into the recesses of hopeless dreams will always be there as a compelling reminder of the "over there" from whence I came. However, a faint light is glimmering as I muse over the parallel to an eye examination. When life's physician asks if it is clearer thru lens A or B, is it A or B? I am beginning to see that the differences are diminishing. Over there will now be here.

The desire for salvation in one form or another is universal. Accepting this notion implies a common path to understanding what it might look like in our everyday lives.

The Creator has endowed us with a seemingly complex, sometimes contradictory, set of emotions that can weave us into the snare of a tangled web. The grand challenge remains, as "peace," the universal metric we've used to measure our success thus far, eludes most of us most of the time.

Things in nature are generally found in balance. Gravitational force is but one elegant example. Too little or too much and we would not be here. Science can and has done much to explain the nuances of how gravity works, but why do we even have gravity? Humans, not always balanced, and can spin out of control emotionally at any time. Like gravity, why we are this way remains a mystery. My suspicion is that if perfection is the desired state, as many sages and gurus insist we strive for, than that would have been achieved by now. Perhaps the answer is far too sublime for us to see.

CHAPTER TWO

DEADWOOD

A h, the sweet smell of success! Yet now that I am
here, the scent isn't quite what I expected. True it is
fresh pine, but I had conjured up something more akin to what
I've already experienced. Perhaps "rest in peace" doesn't
equate to anything I had anticipated or been led to believe.

I park the car in the lot and gaze through bushes to the
fields and mountain beyond with a meandering trail splitting
earth and sky. As I begin walking, I sense this scene has been
created over the millennia. But for whose benefit? Is it for
family, friends, the dog, or me? The simple answer is that it is
available to all who cross its path. Not everyone will notice
everything it has to offer.

It's not long before wild blueberry bushes dance among
the other low vegetation and brush. "Low hanging fruit"
would be regarded as mocking your abilities in some circles,
but here it defines reality. If it's June, the berries will dangle
at your feet just ready to be plucked and sumptuously
squeezed into your mouth. In theory, one should be picking
for the pail, but in reality, that objective only occurs about
half the time.

By hiking standards, this trail is not a difficult trek. It meanders through fields to the tree line, giving way to a noticeably rockier and tree rooted pathway. Even though it's not terribly steep, the trail incorporates switchbacks to enable a hiker to gain elevation gradually. In short order, I am surrounded by the serenity of silence, broken only by what nature has to offer that day. For me, what is most noticeable is the sweet smell of lichen covered scrub pine. A scent "to die for," yet I never had to. I could simply savor the experience from the tapestry woven into my soul for having lived it. Recognizing this insight is one of many scattered throughout our lives just waiting to be picked like those succulent blueberries.

Simple solutions often provide the answer to the most dazzling and perplexing questions we as humans can conjure up in our minds. Could it be that the answer to that most fabled of all dilemmas as to why we are here can be discovered in this way?

Let's take a journey. Mine, yours, ours…

CHAPTER THREE

WHO'S ON FIRST?

A s I suspect with many of us, I live my life through a kaleidoscope of images. Some forgotten, some not yet taken, but others that have shaped who I am and ultimately gave me the insights that helped nurture the core of this book. A cornerstone in my gallery is that of four cows, each with its head in the other cows pasture. Nothing could be more telling than this image, which first captured my imagination as it hung in the window at the college bookstore many years ago. I have lost track of the many careers I have had in fulfilling this vision. Ironically, the ultimate goal of stability was never achieved, much to the loss of my family. One insight gained in these experiences was noting the universal hopes, dreams, triumphs and misfortune we share. No one is immune. There is no way to inoculate ourselves against the onslaught of life except not to live it. A few choose this path, but for most of us, "hope springs eternal." Against all odds, we trudge along, and as Thoreau noted, "live our lives filled with quiet desperation."

Through the millennia, humans have grappled with trying to make sense of our existence. I would posit that it is time to take a collective accounting of our efforts for where they have taken us and where they may lead. The advantage of not being a scholar is that I write what I live, unbound by the constraints of having a particular point of view and then adjusting the facts to fit it. I've learned as much about spirituality and salvation from my stint in sales, another of my core images, as I have from any other career pursuits.

From the time of antiquity, folks charged with our pastoral care have held sway over a good part of our emotional well-being. More often than not, we have had no choice but to believe what they have to say. To have feelings in contrast to belief, whether from the font of secular or spiritual dogma has resulted in the eradication of tens of millions of us.

In today's media saturated world, one would think we are immune to indoctrination and capable of making decisions that are more informed. The collective wisdom of marketing executives would tell you not so fast. They might inform you that spending more money on marketing a product than actually making it will reap the highest rate of return. However, if you think about it, corporations, for all of their success in achieving material wealth, are not very stable relative to life on earth with an average expectancy of sixty years. Less than a mere mortal, dare I say? They are neophytes when it comes to hanging in there for the long run. To find examples at this end of the scale, we must turn to those whose caste is charged with nothing less than our salvation. Saving us from ourselves through some form of spirituality has been around for quite some time, give or take five thousand years if you use Hinduism or its variants as a starting point.

Unrestrained by balance sheets, cash flow statements, and finicky investors, in other words accountable to no one, the world's religions have certainly achieved long life for themselves. Whether they have contributed much in the way of insightful living for us is a mixed bag of achievements and failures. One negative measure would be the tally of accumulated assets held by these entities, ironic in that most hold dear the thought of abandonment of material wealth as one step to enlightenment. One striking respondent to their exhortations was Lady Melania[1] from early antiquity whose annual receipts totaled one hundred twenty thousand pounds of gold around the year 400 A.D. A staggering sum, even if measured by today's standards, qualifying her for a spot on the Forbes list of wealthiest one hundred since the beginning of time. One trusts Lady M and her husband felt a sense of salvation after adopting an acetic lifestyle, coming in vogue in the West as monasticism took hold, as they began giving away their money. We can only hope that the poor among them benefitted, for we know the institutions they supported thrived handily on their largess. The records are rather sketchy, so it is hard to know if they actually gave everything away or salted a few pounds in the cave for a rainy day. They could not avail themselves of trust lawyers and bankers who can create foundations with massive resources that give the semblance of benevolence while insuring tax benefit and control is retained by them or their clients. As I found out through personal experience in work in which I became involved, even if the altruistic motives of donors are sincere, they cannot be assured that their wishes will be fulfilled when they pass on. In this instance, a feeding frenzy at the hands of various asset managers squandered close to $20 million dollars leaving virtually nothing for the beneficiaries of a humanitarian trust.

Grandiloquent[2] is a word I came across that defines the study of theology, at least for me. One requisite attribute for spiritual belief systems is a vocabulary that masks clear meaning for most of us. For example, Sudujaya defines the fifth stage of the Buddhist progress to bodhisattvahood. Explain that and you are well on your way to be able to carry your own among like minded folk.

In Rome, the stationers are quite adept at setting type after centuries of cramming sacred titles onto calling cards. One explanation for the origin of Sufism is it meets the requirements and satisfies the cravings, of a certain class of minds, existing in all ages and in most civilized communities. The evolution of this system of thought should be regarded as a phenomena of spontaneous, independent, and indigenous growth, recurring in many similar and unconnected forms, wherever the human mind continues to concern itself with problems of the wherefore, the whence, and the whither of the Spirit.[3]

One thread, hand in hand with the issue of language, is ascetic practices where giving away wealth as described earlier is but one aspect. All of the major religions have this way of living as an essential component for those seeking a path to enlightenment. We have institutions at the extreme end that offer an eremitic lifestyle to their adherents, thereby allowing them to withdrawn completely from society, perhaps to live in a cave or hut. My personal experience indicates that escapism prevails more than brutal poverty, and insight is not an obvious outcome. These folks are supported in their endeavors by bequeaths and gifts thanks to the largess of the

Lady M's of today. Free from the responsibility of dependants, having no need to own anything as it is provided for, and the ability to pursue personal interests is the rule rather than the exception.

Palden Gyatso[4] in his autobiography related the story of how two different individuals, one a holy man and the other a secular person, faced the death sentence at the hands of Chinese interrogators. In essence, the secular person accepted his fate with the grace and serenity that the holy man had spent a life time cultivating. This example strikes me as giving profound insight to our human experience. Individuals from either camp can learn to live in peace, and the practice of faith in any form does not necessarily equate to learning how to achieve contemplative perfection. In a similar vein, I once had an acquaintance, an ordained Buddhist monk who taught philosophy at a well known college, opine to me that he hated Catholics but admired Mother Theresa. Yes, it is true that those devoted to the sacred life are only human, yet at the time, I was rather perplexed by this hypocritical comment. Today I accept that the lives of these folks, although cast with an aura of wisdom that comes with the rich traditions of their respective faiths, struggle with redemption, for they are on the same journey as the rest of us.

A considerable amount of academic and scholarly talent has been expended over the centuries to expound on the nuances of a given path. Scholars still disagree on the birth of Gautama Buddha[5]. Nothing was written until approximately four hundred years after his estimated death. Let us suppose for a moment that new, definitive evidence arose that placed his death ten years later. Would it make a difference? Not one iota, for I have found the keepers of the various traditions have an uncanny ability to adapt to whatever circumstance arises. Only twenty-eight Buddhas have reached Nirvana, or state of enlightenment. Divide that by several billion adherents and you arrive at a number infinitely small, considerably less than the latest odds of winning Powerball. Great if you're of the religious caste with an infinite pool of candidates; not so good if you're a lowly member of society as you are doomed to endless rebirth no matter how hard you try to reach the pinnacle of your faith journey.

There are roughly nine major categories of religious traditions incorporating a myriad of denominations, practices, and belief systems. Exploring the impact of religion, both positive and negative, on our global society would most likely take several lifetimes. I'm not sure we could even compose a succinct summary, for sacred practices ethereal essence is, by definition, core to its nature, and not subject to quantifiable measurement. To be sure, the contributions to the spiritual dimensions of existence are quite luminous and profound. Less studied, yet just as relevant, is the divisiveness wrought when so many people adhere to so many variants of spirituality, leaving what seems to be irrevocable and irreconcilable sentiments and, of course, as we are all too familiar with, leading to very real wars and staggering intolerance across the globe.

Let's explore a few ways in which the historical record sheds light on how this paradox came to be.

[1] Keeper of the Keys of Heaven, Roger Collins p54
[2] Pompous or extravagant in language, style, or manner, esp. in a way that is intended to impress.
[3] The Asian Journal of Thomas Merton, Glossary
[4] The Autobiography of a Tibetan Monk, Palden Gyatso, p140
[5] L. S. Cousins (1996), "The dating of the historical Buddha: a review article", Journal of the Royal Asiatic Society (3)6(1): 57–63.

CHAPTER 4

NULLITY

A t some point in my literary meanderings, I came across the writings of Leo Tolstoy, not the works he is most noted for, but his writings that focused on his own spiritual quest, one that was to continue until his death. I found the ideas he conveyed, borne from his own personal trials and tribulations, quite insightful for two reasons. First, much of what we know consist of personal accounts as reflected in his diary and letters. I like to be able to sense I'm learning a little about the real person and how he have navigated their own path, not the personae folks might wear as they peddle the latest spiritual solution that will surely ease our pain. Secondly, I found that some of the thoughts that were coagulating in me were already quite similar to what he had expounded on in 1893.[6] I will cover this aspect of his writing a bit later.

Like minded thinking is good and bad, for it's always comforting if someone concurs with us yet it is rather sobering to think that not much has changed in the ensuing century. Tolstoy's seeking led him down varied paths, just like the rest of us. One such expedition led him to the writings of Helchitsky, who penned *Net of Faith* in the fifteenth century. The book was never published; however, Tolstoy eventually purchased the proofs with the aid of a professor with whom he was in correspondence.

Historically, Helchitsky attributes the degeneration of Christianity to the times of Constantine the Great, whom Pope Sylvester admitted into the Christian church with all of his heathen morals and life. Constantine, in his turn, endowed the Pope with worldly riches and power. From this time forward, these two powers were constantly aiding one another for nothing but outward glory. Divines and ecclesiastical dignitaries began to concern themselves only about subduing the whole world to their authority, incited men against one another to murder and plunder, and in creed and in life reduced Christianity to a nullity.

Helchitsky's fundamental idea is that Christianity, by allying itself with temporal power in the days of Constantine and by continuing to develop in such conditions, has been completely distorted ceasing to be Christian altogether. His book derives from the verse of the Gospel about the calling of disciples to be fishers of men. In developing this metaphor, he said,

> *"Christ, by means of his disciples, would have caught the entire world in his net of faith, but the greater fishes broke the net and escaped out of it, and all the rest have slipped through the holes made by the greater fishes, so that the net has remained quite empty. The greater fishes who broke the net were the rulers, emperors, popes, kings, who have not renounced power, and instead of true Christianity have put on what is simply a mask of it."* [7]

We need only to scratch the surface of sacred dogma slightly to realize that much turmoil existing to this day can trace its roots to the forces of theological winds emanating centuries ago. For three of the world's major religions we have Abraham as a cornerstone of their theological wisdom, which could be viewed as problematic given his resume. No wonder we struggle in the twenty first century to live by standards with roots tracing back to a somewhat nefarious character who himself often did not live by the rules ultimately laid down for the rest of us. Of course, we could argue that his well rounded demeanor allows for the many interpretations we have over nuanced meanings contained in the Koran, Bible or Torah.

In one interpretation, Abraham had a son, Ishmael, by Hagar, his concubine, given that Sarah, his wife, was barren. Sarah, ticked off, wanted both Hagar and Ishmael killed. Then, a greater revenge occurred when Sarah herself, perhaps in hers 90's, had a child by Abraham, Isaac. God then tested Abraham by telling him to sacrifice Isaac on the pyre at Moriah. Abraham, a mercenary by trade, one not accustomed to trusting anyone, decided he will follow the will of God, and as he readied to execute his son, God relented. "I'm only kidding dear chap. It was only a test." Phew, a nation was on its way after a rocky start.

"What about me?" Ishmael asked. "Don't I get a nation?" Historical weaving continues as Abraham, already having achieved what he wanted, left Hagar and Ishmael in the desert near Mecca. God, however, took care of them by revealing the sacred spring of Zamzam to quench their thirst. Abraham reappeared and together with Ishmael, happily reunited although abandoned, built the Kaaba, the most sacred site in

Islam. Now Ishmael had his nation as father to the Arabs. As conveyed in the Qur'an, although it's not always obvious today, the concept of non-Muslim faiths accorded a certain respect as being "People of the Book" is rooted in this divine revelation.

Just as the trickledown theory of Reaganomics failed, so too much of what we see played out in the "theatre of operations" in the Middle East today can be traced to scripts written eons ago. Fact or fanciful, these transcribed thoughts that have made it into holy books have very real consequences. When Muhammad suddenly died in 632, the khalifa (his successor), was his close aide and friend Abu Bakr. Dissidents felt that only a direct descendant, Ali ibn Abi Talib, his son-in-law and cousin should replace him. He later did as the fourth caliph. However, the rift never healed and we have seen the Shi'a and Sunni struggle played out in the Iraq war and beyond.

In 1929, Pope Pius XI signed an accord with the fascist dictator, Benito Mussolini. Called the Lateran Treaty, it laid the framework for the Vatican City we know today and other property remnants from the legacy of the Papal States. In fact, when Popes, including the Francis of today, need a respite from the toils of shepherding the flock, they stay at Castel Gandolfo, one of these properties ceded to the Church in this pact.

In return, Mussolini had obtained many benefices, one being the suppression of the Italian People's Party in 1923, well before the signing in 1929. Of interest, this party was co-founded by a priest named Luigi Sturzo in 1919[8], a committed anti-fascist.

Proponents of one faith path use the fodder of history to expound upon the virtues of their own particular point of view as a clear alternative to the "corrupt" institution in their gun sites. Martin Luther would fit into this category. Obviously, he struck a chord with what he preached, for he soon had many adherents, which ultimately led to a great schism and a new Christian denomination. If we fast forward to today, his legacy has come under greater scrutiny. One example of the many criticisms that have become known is his advising an individual to marry a second woman without first divorcing his first. His judgment might have gone unnoticed had it not been for the fact that he was counseling Philip I, Landgrave of Hesse. In other words, he was a member of the ruling caste, and Protestants have fragmented into a myriad of denominations, each once again expounding its own virtues.

Tibet, known as the "Roof of the World", is the highest region on earth averaging sixteen thousand feet in elevation. The allure of its culture and its mountains has attracted a considerable following around the world, yet it was essentially a feudal society for centuries with a rigid social structure and caste system made up of lay folks, nobility, and monks. A small wealthy minority ruled the country while landless "untouchables" made up the lowest class. The Chinese were often used these facts in their propaganda as they began sweeping through the country in 1959.

Monastic influence is so pervasive in this country that it really is difficult to distinguish the secular from sacred. I, like many folks, particularly in the West, was drawn to the plight of the Tibetan people as they fought to maintain their independence from China. However, over time, I have come to believe that the real Tibet is shrouded in mystery far greater than the lofty peaks that surround it. Because of extreme political volatility in the region, it is virtually impossible to get objective information about the country. Most historians spend more time trying to discredit the opposition than shed light on their subject. If you don't believe me, simply type in "objective facts on Tibet" in any search engine and you will soon see that the factoid creators are divided evenly between Tibetan and Chinese support groups. If you simply want to know the illiteracy rate, say in the 1920's, you will have to search long and hard to find it.

I do not in any way support what China has done to suppress and subdue the country, including ravaging the countryside and torturing its citizens. In fact, I refer to Palden Gayatso in this book; I admire what he has done for his people, and for his courage under circumstances that would crush most of us. I will leave that story for others to continue to tell as the new Tibet succumbs under the weight of the so called autonomous rule.

Just as I explored early papal history, my trek into Tibet has taken me on a journey in an attempt to peer beyond the veil of theology that shrouds its culture. I want to get a clearer sense of its monastic legacy that not only encompasses the compassionate point of view offered in the West but also provides some insights in to the rather dark side, making it hard to reconcile with what is preached. Like the nullity of Christianity, Tibetan Buddhism has treated much of its citizenry with an almost paternal air consistent with the feudal system of governance that had been in place for hundreds of years. In the case of Tibetan citizens, many in the monastic orders extol the virtue of the peasant class, indicating that they much preferred it to what exists today. Perhaps so, but if the majority of them can't read, have little or no education, and were tied for eternity to serfdom, it stands to reason that this situation does not represent an enlightened path of existence. If we were speaking of Haiti, Bangladesh, or a myriad of other countries, the international community would be exposing this state of affairs as a denial of basic human rights.

After some period of reviewing biased interpretations of one sort or another, I finally ran across the work of Melvyn C. Goldstein. His writings and analysis represent excellence in good scholarship. Leave personal bias out of the documentary history and let readers formulate their own opinions as to what really occurred. The following is one excerpt of Goldstein's work, giving us an overview of the estate system that existed.[9]

In Tibet, estates (tib. Shiga) could be held by aristocratic families, monasteries, incarnate lamas, or the government itself. Such estates were granted by the ruler (the Dalai Lama or regent) who had the right to confiscate such estates and occasionally did so, although in reality the estate holders held their land hereditarily across generations. The Tibetan ruler also had the right to grant new estates, as he did for the families of the new dalai lamas, thus ennobling them and making them part of the lay aristocracy.

Tibet's estates combined the means of production-economically productive land-with a hereditarily bound peasant labor force. The estate's land was made up of two sections: the lord's land and the peasants land. The lord's land typically constituted about one-half to three-fourths of the total arable land on the estate and was cultivated entirely by the estate's hereditarily bound peasants as a corvee obligation (tib. ula), that is, as a labor tax with no reimbursement. On most estates, peasant families had to provide their lord one worker every day and two or more at peak agricultural times. If there was no agricultural work to be done, the lord could have his corvee workers do other things, such as collect firewood or spin wool. The entire yield from the land went directly to the lord. The remainder of the estate's land was allocated to the estate's hereditarily bound peasants and was the means by which they derived their subsistence. They did not own the land in the sense of having the right to sell it, but they normally held usufruct rights so long as their corvee obligations were fulfilled. The defining feature of the Tibetan estate system was that the peasants did not have the right to relinquish their land and seek their fortunes elsewhere. They were not free; they belonged to their estate hereditarily, and if they ran away, the lord had the right to pursue and forcibly return them to the estate.

The authority of estates over their peasants was political as well as economic. Lords adjudicated disputes, meted out punishments, and controlled the movement of their peasants. The permanent, subservience-bound status of peasants to their estates/lords was manifest clearly when individuals sought to leave their estate permanently. For example, to marry a person from a different estate or to join a monastery required permission from the lord.

In marriage, the simplest method of securing such permission was via person exchange (tib. mije). This practice involved marrying out with someone marrying in from the other estate. Another common practice for handling an out-marrying situation involved the brides or grooms leasing their physical freedoms from the estate by paying a fee which was called "human lease"(tib. mibo) in perpetuity to their lords.

Human lease status fees varied significantly in size and nature. The fee was typically money, but sometimes also labor or goods, or even both. Lords kept detailed records of their subjects, including household births and deaths and annual human lease payments. In essence, therefore, virtually the entire Tibetan peasantry was hereditarily tied to estates/lords either directly or through human lease status.

Monks and nuns, however, were partly an exception to this practice. Peasants seeking to become monks or nuns required the permission of their lord which was invariably granted. As long as the peasants remained in the monastic order, they had no obligations to the estate/lord. The authority of lords over their subjects also included the right to transfer them unilaterally to other individuals, both other lords and rich peasants, although this practice was not common in Tibet. Lords could also physically move their peasants to other locations in accordance with their own labor requirements. An example of this situation occurred in the late 1940s on one of Drepung Monastery's estates. Drepung required large quantities of firewood for the daily mangja tea to serve its ten thousand monks and decided to use its corvee peasant force to provide this labor at no cost to the monastery. It did so by moving twelve young unmarried men from one of the monasteries estates to a noncontiguous mountain area, where they lived in tents and were responsible for cutting and transporting firewood for a ten-year period. These youths were drafted on the basis of their families' obligations to provide corvee labor to the lord; therefore, they received no salary or food during the ten years the monastery kept them there, although their families did receive credit for providing one corvee laborer per day to the estate. The peasant households, of course, did not have the option to refuse to send their son for this task.[10]

The Tibetan political economy, therefore, not only provided elites with productive resources but also critically guaranteed them a "captive" labor force. From the lord's vantage point, this practice was an extremely efficient system that required minuscule expenditures of their money or time. Lords did not have to compete for workers in a labor market, nor did they have to worry about the feeding, clothing, and housing of the workers as in a slavery system. The lord's role, played by an incarnate lama, a monastery, an aristocrat, or the government itself, needed only to supply a manager or steward to organize the hereditarily bound labor force on its estate.

Finally, the fact that virtually the entire peasantry was hereditarily bound to an estate and lord did not mean the peasantry was homogeneous in terms of standard of living and status; various estate classes held different rights and obligations. Consequently, being a serf, a bound peasant did not necessarily mean poverty. Many taxpayer families were actually wealthy and had their own servants.

In summary, the Tibetan feudal political-economic system was based on estates, each of which had hereditarily bound serfs who provide free labor and often taxes in kind. The monasteries, incarnate lamas, aristocrats, and the government itself all depended on this system of relations.[11]

What are we to make of this depiction of Tibetan life? We've all heard of the adage that power corrupts and absolute power corrupts absolutely. We are drawn to the magnetism of a voice that offers hope on our journey. Like minded individuals gather and before they know it, an institutional framework is created to manage the individual fervor. Over time, these entities suffer from the same maladies as they had hoped to escape. I have come to believe that by seeking solace in group think, we abdicate our individual responsibilities. Institutions have and will continue to add to the common good, but they are also quite capable of doing bad. Our individual salvation may have little to do with what is good for the church, city, state, or synagogue to survive.

It strikes me that the majority of stories that capture our imagination and inspire us are those that spring from the well of the individual. Without Pietro di Bernardone, there are no Franciscans; without Siddhārtha Gautama there are no Buddhists; without Muḥammad ibn `Abd Allāh there are no Muslims; without Christ there are no Christians; without Anjezë Gonxhe Bojaxhiu there are no Missionaries of Charity; and without Mírzá Ḥusayn-`Alí Núrí there are no Bahá'í.

In summary, we acknowledge the great gifts that individuals have imparted to the world as evidenced in the expansive institutions left in their wake. On the other hand, these institutions have to be cognizant of the fact that what they are now may in no way reflect the legacy upon which they were built. They should strive to eliminate the barriers to understanding that they themselves have created. The only way this transformation can happen is if they subject themselves to the same exacting scrutiny laid down for the rest of us. Graced with humility to subdue their will to be right, they would then be able to carry out their missions, just as we as individuals strive to do in our everyday lives. We

will explore this notion further in this book, for it may hold a
critical clue on our quest.

---

6 The Kingdom of God is Within You, Leo Tolstoy, translated by
   Constance Garnett
7 Ibid, p.18
8 Farrell-Vinay, Giovanna. 2004. The London Exile of Don Luigi
   Sturzo (1924-1940). *HeyJ*. XLV, pp. 158-177.
9 Modern Tibetan History, Vol. 2: The Estate System, Melvyn C.
   Goldstein[University of California Press; Berkeley, Los Angeles,
   London. 2007.]
10 Samdrup (interview, 1989, Lhasa, Tibet Autonomous Region,
   China). Samdrup was a monk working under the overall manager
   of Drepung (tib. jiso) and was personally in charge of this
   operation.
11 Modern Tibetan History, Vol. 2: The Estate System, Melvyn C.
   Goldstein[University of California Press; Berkeley, Los Angeles,
   London. 2007.]

CHAPTER 5

EXTREME MAKEOVERS

Individual initiative has not always led to a new religion. Some folks sensed their redemptive callings would best be served by leading a life of extreme mortification. I wonder what Simeon Stylites the Elder would make of cell phone technology. Simeon climbed a pillar in Syria in 423 A.D. and stayed there until his death thirty seven years later. Perhaps the familiar quip of Verizon marketing gurus had its origins back to Simeon's ground crew. The response to "Can you hear me now?" would have been a good measure of wind gusts on any given day.

Baradatus lived in the fifth century in the Syrian Desert. He built a small lattice, coffin-like structure made of interwoven pieces of wood. It was fashioned in such a way that it had many openings, so as to be open to all the conditions of the weather. It in no way conformed to the dimensions of a human body, but one in which he had to live bent double, for neither its depth nor its length was of a convenient size. He spent ten years this way, and considering he was a rather large, fat man when he entered the cell, we may easily conjecture how he felt and how he looked.

Devout as Baradatus was, when Theodotus, Bishop of Antioch at this time, showed up and saw the conditions in which he was living, he ordered him to come out of the enclosure and to serve God in other ways.

Out of the coffin, Baradatus continued to labor for the sake of his and the world's salvation. The desire for penance made him devise an even more painful form of worship. Having weaved a body suite out of leather, he put it on and was completely covered from head to toe, with only openings for the nose and mouth so as to breathe. He could not even see.[12]

I often wonder if ascetics compared shop notes to determine who carried the day with respect to pushing the limits on torturous penance for bad behavior, real or imagined. Thalaleus must have been near the top of his game when he prepared himself two wheels, each two cubits or about three and a half feet in diameter. He then connected these wheels by nailing boards to the rims at intervals all round in order to make the wheels stand one cubit apart the board being fastened by one end to the upper wheel and the other end to the lower like the rungs of a double cogwheel. He then set in the ground three tall pieces of timber connected at the top by three cross pieces so as to stand firmly with their lower ends farther apart than the upper. Within this frame, he suspended his double wheel into which he then squeezed himself. Having a space of only two cubits wide and one cubit high he had to bend himself double with his chin touching his knees in this position.[13]

Sivapuri Baba reportedly lived for 137 years. He was born in 1826, married at approximately fourteen, and had two sons and two daughters. At age twenty-two, flush with wealth inherited from his grandfather, he left his family and entered the woods where he lived for the next twenty-five years. Close to age fifty, he emerged and began a world tour that would take forty years to complete for he travelled on foot. He became the personal yoga master to Queen Victoria and travelled to the west meeting Theodore Roosevelt.

Baba's core teaching revolved around three principal duties. First, a physical duty, consisting mainly in maintaining one's body and mind through proper livelihood, and helping your dependents do the same. Second was a moral duty that consisted in remaining sensitive to the obligation to seek the truth twenty four hours a day. Third, a spiritual duty meant the worship of the Divine. It is ironic that like many others before him, he broke one of these sacred tenets in order to obtain his enlightened state.

These feats of willful determination and self-control, along with many of a similar nature, makes extreme sports seem like toddler play. It is interesting to note that quite often "extreme suffering" is a spectator sport. I suspect it's that pesky ego that once again bests us. Who would know of my suffering if I endure it alone? Again, I've asked myself this question over and over and have reconsidered my attempts to make sense of the many ways people have explored how to best achieve redemption. I can assure the reader that a crypt provides a simple solution. There are no calling birds, turtledoves, or loathsome humans. Absolute, total, infinite silence is yours. Not even a pin dropping or scratching of rodents to worry about in that environment.

For obvious reasons, relatively few folks have chosen asceticism in the last few centuries, and interest in this approach has waned. Buddha, in a measure of his wisdom, made a mid-course correction in his spiritual journey after realizing extreme asceticism did not lead to enlightenment. There are exceptions, even today, as exemplified by Hindu sects that live the life of a sadhu, or wandering monk. It is interesting to note that caste still plays a role in whether or not one is admitted to some of these sects.

As a counterpoint, extreme opulence is alive and well, seemingly surging as asceticism diminishes. The chefs at the Emirates Palace in Dubai spend $300,000 annually on solid gold pastry decorations.[14] I am certain I could fill a large book cataloguing similar exploits that occur in just one day around the planet as Bob Harris did for Forbes magazine. Unfortunately, the extremely poor of today do not muster the same shock and awe that the ascetics of the middle ages attempted to instill in those who displayed this same kind of extravagance in their own time.

However, what Bob did with the money he received for his story stands as a small but extraordinary witness to an individual rewriting his legacy without climbing a pillar. I'll detail more on his initiative a bit later in the book.

---

[12] History of the Christian Church Volumes 1 & 11, William Jones, 1819, p376

[13] The Fathers of the Desert, Volume 2, Henry Ruffner, 1850, p228

[14] Book review by Megan Woolhouse on Bob Harris's, "The International Bank of Bob", Boston Globe, March 15, 2013

CHAPTER 6

MONEYED WATERS

If you haven't already figured it out, my natural environment plays a major role in my own life. At this moment, I'm hiking a trail that straddles the proverbial babbling brook as it moves up to the quintessential waterfall. Not Niagara Falls, but it is a sufficiently enjoyable scene to behold. I am sharing this local wonder with one of my daughters and that in itself is enough, right? Dare I say peaceful with no multilevel meditation required? And the noise from the falls as it roars over the rock formations is a sound I'm fortunate to hear.

Registries of waterfalls worldwide can now be found online. And guess what? They are not categorized by denomination. Imagine that. Waterfalls share similar attributes everywhere in the world, and if you think about it so do trees, flowers, oceans, birds, etc., etc.

The Creator endowed our planet with many wonders. From magnificent beauty to enchant us, to rich natural resources to sustain us, and immeasurable complexity for us to sort out, there is much to behold. Of course, there is much to torment us as well. It is interesting to note that except in the human species, salvation is not very relevant. I am unaware of a tree, asking the tree next to it to shut off its water supply deliberately so it could die a noble death to atone for its life. Granted, certain species can and will overrun their neighbor if they are more adapted to a particular environment.

Legend has it that this trail takes its name from counterfeiters milling out Spanish dollars. Their tools were discovered by a hunter, and their operation was shut down. There's no absolute connection, but one Caleb Gardiner was tried and hung for passing these counterfeit dollars. Swift justice as it was known by back then. Of course, it involved money, and offenses against the holy grail of commerce would move any offender to the top of the justice list. It has been said, "Money is the root of all evil." I would opine that the control over another that the money buys as the main culprit. Our having free will as part of our DNA has caused considerable havoc with most of us.

The term "social justice" is a mainstay of our dialogue in the twenty first century. Way back in the third century, we find yet another voice railing against the tidal wave of servitude that marks each generations passing. John Chrysostom, born in Antioch around 347 AD, picked up the torch to rail against the status quo of his day. He was ultimately exiled, dying en route to his destiny, much like Tolstoy. As with Helchitsky in the fifteenth century, he identified the Emperor's Constantine endorsement of Christianity as a major turning point in its history. Given its tumultuous past up to then, the stability that this secular blessing offered to Christianity came at a hefty price, but one the liturgical hierarchy was willing to accept for it certainly insured their survival.

John was born to a family of wealthy aristocrats (no surprise here), and throughout his life he exuded the self-assurance that his upbringing gave him. He learned the art of legal rhetoric under the great pagan orator Libanius, but in 368 AD, he renounced his career as advocate, received baptism, and then devoted himself to studying Scriptures. He felt compelled by the teachings of Christ to give away his wealth, and for a period he went to live as a hermit in a cave. He eventually returned to Antioch where he was ordained a priest.

During the following ten years, John delivered a sermon at least once a week. Although he sometimes tackled theological subjects, he persistently returned to the subject of justice. He argued that rich people should see themselves as stewards of their wealth, lent to them by God to be used for the common good. In the most vehement language, he denounced those who live in luxury without thought for the poor. His most stinging invective language was for those who made conspicuous displays of generosity to the church, buying new chalices and robes for the priests, yet ignoring the beggars at their gates. He saw the Eucharist as a symbol for the political and moral values he proclaimed.

In 389 AD, when the old patriarch died, the Emperor invited John to fill the post because of his popularity and his pedigree. He set about his new task with unrelenting energy, increasing the number of schools and hospitals run by the church and rooting out corruption among clergy. He frequently visited slums, going on foot and talking to people along the way. He continued to preach, accusing the rich of insulting God himself by their greed.

As you can imagine, in spite of his familial legacy, opposition to his ministry grew. Empress Eudoxia, who exemplified all that John loathed, urged her husband to expel him. A large section of the clergy also voiced their anxieties, and they were backed by the patriarch of Alexandria, who was jealous of John's fame. A synod of bishops and clergy convened, and John was found guilty and deposed, with the threat of exile if he continued to preach. The people of the city were outraged, and he was reinstated to prevent riots, but two months later, he preached a sermon that the Empress interpreted-perhaps rightly-as directed against her. At her insistence, he was abducted while he was celebrating Communion at Easter.

Initially, he was taken to a small town in Armenia, but the bishops decided that his death was the only means of ensuring peace. They persuaded the Emperor to order John to be taken to a fortress at the eastern end of the Black Sea. He was compelled to travel on foot during the autumn rains, wearing only a few rags. He died on the journey, with the words "Glory to God for everything" on his lips. He was age sixty.[15]

Given the propensity for humans to want to control one another rather than live and let live, I do not believe secular options provide much in the way of a path toward salvation either. My own observation and experience has informed my thinking that capitalism cultivates amoral behavior in its wake, leaving the corporate class blameless for whatever befalls the hapless citizens of the country in which they operate.

I do not understand why we idolize the rich who make donations and bequests from monies that might have been more equitably distributed to their employees. Again, one does not have to mine historical records very deeply to find that much of the largess of the rich has ended up in sacred hands. Is one hand washing the other?

---

[15] On Living Simply (1997), the Golden Voice of John Chysostom, Robert Van De Weyer, Introduction

.

CHAPTER 7

TANTALUS

The toiling masses, the immense majority of mankind who are suffering under the incessant, meaningless, and hopeless toil and privation in which their whole life is swallowed up, still find their keenest suffering in the glaring contrast between what is and what ought to be, according to all the beliefs held by themselves and those who have brought them to that condition and keep them in it.

They know they are in slavery and condemned to privation and darkness in order to minister to the lusts of the minority who keep them down. This knowledge increases their sufferings and constitutes its bitterest sting.

The slave of antiquity knew that he was a slave by nature, but our laborer, while he feels he is a slave, knows that he ought not to be, so he tastes the agony of Tantalus, forever desiring and never gaining what might and ought to be his.[16]

One would hope a spiritual sage had characterized the human condition from an economic perspective so adroitly, but that task was left to a secular Tolstoy in 1893. Of the many writers I have encountered, he is one of the few who make the direct and searing connection between our economic and spiritual wellbeing. This gulf continues to widen today as we now even have "right to work" legislative initiatives sponsored by corporations with silent acquiescence from our religious institutions, tasked with countering the onslaught of economic malfeasance. There is plenty of hypocrisy to go around as many in leadership roles, both sacred and secular, hold their flock and employees to a standard much higher than their own. Find a religious working alongside Foxconn assemblers in China, and you have the makings of a saint.

In his work, "Confessions," Tolstoy delves into the same paradox that still exists today in that what is meant to unite us ultimately divides.

In spite of my doubts and sufferings I still clung to the Orthodox Church, but questions about life arose that had to be decided, and the decision of these questions by the Church, contrary to the very bases of the belief by which I lived, obliged me at last to renounce communion with Orthodoxy as impossible. The first question was the relation of the Orthodox Eastern Church to other Churches, to the Catholics, and to the so-called sectarians. At that time, in consequence of my interest in religion, I came into touch with believers of various faiths: Catholics, Protestants, Old-Believers, Molokans[17], and others. I met among them many men of lofty morals who were truly religious; I wished to be a brother to them. What happened? That teaching which promised to unite all in one faith and love, that very teaching, in the person of its best representatives, told me that these men were all living a lie, that what gave them their power of life was a temptation of the devil and that we alone possess the only possible truth.

I saw that all who do not profess an identical faith with themselves are considered by the Orthodox to be heretics, just as the Catholics and others consider the Orthodox to be heretics. I also saw that the Orthodox (though they try to hide this fact) regard with hostility all who do not express their faith by the same external symbols and words as themselves. This circumstance arises naturally. First, because the assertion that you are in falsehood, and I am in truth, is the most cruel thing one man can say to another, and secondly, because a man loving his children and brothers cannot help being hostile to those who wish to pervert his children and brothers to a false belief. That hostility is increased in proportion to one's greater knowledge of theology, and to me who considered that truth lay in union by love, it became self-evident that theology was itself destroying what it ought to produce.

Drawing this conclusion is so obvious to us educated people who have lived in countries where various religions are professed. We have seen the contempt, self-assurance, and invincible contradiction with which Catholics behave to the Orthodox Greeks and to the Protestants, and the Orthodox to Catholics and Protestants, the Protestants to the two others, the Old-Believers, Pashkovites (Russian Evangelicals), Shakers, and all religions so that the very obviousness of this situation at first perplexes us. One says to oneself that it is impossible that it is so simple and that people do not see that if two assertions are mutually contradictory, then neither of them has the sole truth that faith should possess.

There is something else here; there must be some explanation. I thought there was, and sought that explanation and read all I could on the subject, and consulted all whom I could. No one, however, gave me any explanation, except the one that causes the Sumsky Hussars to consider the Sumsky Hussars the best regiment in the world and the Yellow Uhlans to consider that the best regiment in the world is the Yellow Uhlans. The ecclesiastics of all the different creeds, through their best representatives, told me nothing but that they believed themselves to have the truth and the others to be in error, and that all they could do was to pray for them.

I went to archimandrites, bishops, elders, and monks of the strictest orders and asked them to explain this paradox but none of them did so except one man, who explained it all and explained it so that I never asked anyone any more about it. I said that for every unbeliever turning to a belief (and all our young generation are in a position to do so), the question that presents itself first is why is truth not in Lutheranism nor in Catholicism, but in Orthodoxy? Educated in the high school, he cannot help knowing what the peasants do not know: the Protestants and Catholics equally affirm that their faith is the only true one. Historical evidence, twisted by each religion in its own favor is insufficient. "Is it not possible," said I, "to understand the teaching in a loftier way, so that from its height the differences should disappear, as they do for one who truly believes?

Can we not go further along a path like the one we are following with the Old-Believers? They emphasized the fact that they have a differently shaped cross and different alleluias and a different procession round the altar. We reply, "You believe in the Nicene Creed, in the seven sacraments, and so do we. Let us hold to that, and in other matters, do as you please." We have united with them by placing the essentials of faith above the inessentials. Now with the Catholics can we not say, "You believe in so and so and in so and so, which are the chief things, and as for the Filioque clause and the Pope, do as you please." Can we not say the same to the Protestants, thereby uniting with them in what is most important?[18]

My interlocutor agreed with my thoughts, but told me that such conceptions would bring reproach from the spiritual authorities for deserting the faith of our forefathers. This condition would produce a schism, and the vocation of the spiritual authorities is to safeguard in all its purity the Greco-Russian Orthodox faith inherited from our forefathers.

I now understood my dilemma. I am seeking a faith, the power of life, and they are seeking the best way to fulfill in the eyes of men certain human obligations. And in fulfilling these human affairs, they do so in a human way. However much they may talk of their pity for their erring brethren and of addressing prayers for them to the throne of the Almighty, violence will, if necessary, been and will be applied. If of two religions each considers itself true and the other false, then men desiring to attract others to the truth will preach their own doctrine. If a false teaching is preached to the inexperienced sons of their church as the truth, then that church must burn the books and remove the man who is misleading its sons. What is to be done with a sectarian, burning, in the opinion of the Orthodox, with the fire of false doctrine, who in the most important affair of life, in faith, misleads the sons of the church? What can be done with him except to cut off his head or to incarcerate him? Under the Tsar Alexis Mikhaylovich people were burned at the stake, that is to say, the severest method of punishment of the time was applied, and in our day also the severest method of punishment is applied, detention in solitary confinement.

The second relation of the church to a question of life was with regard to war and executions. At that time Russia was at war, and Russians, in the name of Christian love, began to kill their fellow men. It was impossible not to think about this predicament, and not to see that killing is an evil repugnant to the first principles of any faith. However, prayers were said in the churches for the success of our arms, and the teachers of the Faith acknowledged killing to be an act resulting from the Faith. Besides the murders during the war, I saw, during the disturbances that followed the war, church dignitaries and teachers and monks of the lesser and stricter orders who approved the killing of helpless, erring youths. I took note of all that is done by men who profess Christianity, and I was horrified.[19]

In summary, Tolstoy felt that theologians had failed in alleviating the plight of Tantalus for the indentured class. However, he developed a rigid outlook, and as I have experienced, being certain that your point of view is correct is usually a tip off that it's not. If it's that difficult to follow one's proposed alternative path, then how likely is to be that simple, elegant solution we all seek? It doesn't appear that Tolstoy ever really came to terms with his own wealth, his obligations to his family, and his troubled relationship with his wife. After finally determining to leave all behind and become a wandering ascetic, he died from pneumonia within days after boarding a train en route to his destiny.

One thing Tolstoy did for humanity was to ensure in his death that he would accomplish what he found elusive when he was alive: to make some tangible statement that expressed his beliefs distilled from his lifetime search for redemption.

One way he accomplished this act of salvation, much to the distress of some heirs, was the desire to have his writings forever to remain in the public domain.

To wit, one draft of his will: "Herewith I declare that I desire those of my compositions, literary productions, and writings of every kind, whether published or unpublished, which have been written, or have attained first publication, since the first day of January 1881, as also those of them which were written previously thereto, but have not yet attained publication, to constitute, after my death, no person's private property, but to be freely publishable and republishable by all who may desire so to use them. I desire that all manuscripts and documents extant at the time of my death shall be handed to Vladimir Grigoryevich Tchertkoff, to the end that, after my decease, he may dispose of them as heretofore, and that they may be freely accessible to all who may desire to make use of them for publication. I request Vladimir Grigoryevich Tchertkoff to select such person or persons as, in the event of his decease, he may entrust with the fulfillment of these my behests. Leo Nikolayevoch Tolstoy, Krekshino, September 18th, 1909."[20]

Gustavo Gutierrez spent his life articulating a similar point of view in his writing and lectures ultimately leading to what has been called "liberation theology." For Gutierrez, Utopia refers to "a personal transformation by which we live with profound inner freedom in the face of every kind of servitude."[21] This involved a three-fold process, which embraces 1) the creation of a just and humane socioeconomic and political order, 2) the emancipation of human consciousness from self-concern and 3) redemption by God from sin for a communion of love.

Guiterrez's work directly confronted institutional apathy, both secular and sacred, or "nullity" as defined earlier, yet central to his message was a hope that the individual would, and in some cases had in Latin America, rise above one's lot as evidence of the reality of his theories.

Predictably, he was admonished by the Congregation of the Faith in 1984 and 1986 by then Cardinal Ratzinger, now retired Pope Benedict the XIV, as he considered this movement to be aligned too closely with Marxism. To me, the only connection is that they both articulated the plight of the poor but for entirely different reasons. Marx was an economist and Gutierrez a theologian. Marx offered solutions that had mass appeal, thereby creating a feeding frenzy for despots to seize upon. He provided the true "opiate of the masses" to corrupt demagogues that now knew they had a new stealth weapon by offering economic salvation to everyone in the ultimate Ponzi scheme. In capitalism, one knows the wealthiest expect to have even more. In communism, accumulating wealth is taboo yet embraced. The Forbes China 400 Rich list reveals that over 90% of the 1,000 richest people tracked by the Hurun Report are either officials or members of the Chinese Communist Party. Well, so much for Mao's Little Red Book.

Gutierrez, on the other hand, saw rich and poor as intimately tied to the ultimate struggle for peace and salvation on our earthly journeys. However, he did expend much time to explaining his view of adhering to Marxist theory as far its ability to articulate the ills of capitalism while being opposed to Marxism, for it was implemented in a totalitarian fashion.

These differences, as in the past, provide much fodder for the intellectual elite as they parse the harsh reality in determining the best ways to lord over the masses. Eventually over time, the Church has been reevaluating its position, for at its pinnacle, Gutierrez's writings harkens the "institution" to reflect on its true mission emanating from its founder a long, long time ago.

At the same time, Gutierrez, as the erudite scholar that he was, expended a staggering amount of his intellectual capacity in finding a biblically proscribed explanation for his point of view, thereby opening up yet another one of those tacit theological barriers that others had or will continue to refute. In the end, divisiveness is on par with any enlightenment that might be offered.

After reading and researching similar writings from many learned individuals, it occurred to me that what they offered hadn't changed the hearts and minds of as many as they had hoped. One thing I noted is that throughout the centuries, we often tie redemption with helping the poor. This connection bothered me, for over the years I couldn't help but feel a disconnection when I was asked to contribute to a multitude of charities and then go about my business. What was going on in my heart was never challenged. Historically, so many had found redemption by given up their life of wealth to serve the poor. Noble yes, but I never heard of one giving up poverty to be rich.

I began to sense that perhaps alleviating poverty and redemption may or may not be connected as we had been led to believe. Let's explore why this might be the case.

16 The Kingdom of God is Within You, Leo Tolstoy, p69

17 A sect that rejects sacraments and ritual.

18 A Confession, Leo Tolstoy, 1882, XV

19 A Confession, Leo Tolstoy, 1882, XV

20 The Diary of Leo Tolstoy p 227, translated from the Russian by C. J. Hogarth

21 Theology of Liberation, xxxviii

CHAPTER 8

EQUITY SHARING

If you had not eaten for days, and I offered you .111% of my pie or 99.889%, which piece would most likely satisfy your appetite? Voodoo economists would convince you that the miniscule amount represented by the former would most certainly satiate your hunger. And right out of Houdini's hat, we would accept this stupendous lie as fact, for it's hard to quibble with details when you're about to keel over dead from starvation.

Rounding off the numbers, 81% of the world's wealth is in the hands of .1% of the population, leaving 19% for the remaining 99.9% to divvy up.[22] Also of note is the fact that religious affiliation, including none at all, seems to have little bearing on the urge of the wealthiest to rethink their lot as the top ten billionaires include an atheist, two agnostics, three Christians, two Catholics, and two Hindus.[23]

The well-known phrase "Life, Liberty, and the Pursuit of Happiness" from our Declaration of Independence, although written with noble intent, seems to have little basis in reality, for the vast majority of people in the world live in an impoverished state with little time to contemplate the meaning of life. A rough estimate is that there are three billion of us living on less than $2.50 per day.[24] The reason I am speaking to this issue in this book is to differentiate between a spiritual path and a basic human right. As I mentioned earlier, ascetics choose poverty rather than have it being proscribed by birth. Bending one's will to greater fulfillment is of little consequence if the belly is unnourished.

In my humble opinion, there are two choices available to address this cultural malignancy. One is to consider the existence of poverty as a reflection of the "Poverty of the Soul" in the minds and hearts of the wealthiest citizens, and we would therefore, seek solutions that would lift them out of their impoverished state. This task would seemingly fit in with one of the roles of theology. Much scripture of any faith persuasion is devoted to sensitizing their respective flocks to the neediest, and more importantly, that pursuing material wealth is of little consequence in this life or any hereafter. Perhaps by focusing on those bastions of industry or government rather than the physically poor, their efforts might lead these folks to make better choices in allocating resources under their purvey. Maybe they have improved and the institutions they lead would be much worse than they are without the prodding. However, because of the nullity effect I touched on earlier, the status quo will hold the day to ensure institutional survival. I suspect that the reason the billions of dollars spent to eradicate poverty have not succeeded is that the collective will is not there to alter our hearts. The key is to view the poor just like anyone who is not, which of course they are, and not to assume they exist to provide existential benefits to those in circumstances that are more fortunate.

The other option is to cultivate economic solutions that allow the poor to help themselves regardless of faith persuasion. Distribution of wealth in a social democratic fashion offers the realistic opportunity to achieve these desired results. This redistribution, at its best, is not achieved through handouts but by creatively extending economic opportunity to all members of a society. Mohammed Yunus, founder of Grameen Bank in Bangladesh, gives us a perfect opportunity to see how this idea works in action. He simply started giving small, uncollateralized loans to impoverished individuals so that they could develop small businesses to generate cash for their families.

He was inspired during the terrible Bangladesh famine of 1974 to make a small loan of $27.00 to a group of 42 families so that they could create small items for sale without the burdens of predatory lending. He believes that charity is not an answer to poverty. It creates dependency and takes away an individual's initiative to break through the cycle of poverty, whereas loans offer people the opportunity to take initiatives in business or agriculture, thereby providing earnings and enabling them to pay off the debt. This ideology regards all human beings, including the poorest, as endowed with endless potential, and that unleashing the creativity in each individual should be the answer to poverty. Grameen has offered credit to many poor, women, illiterate and unemployed people.

Grameen Bank does ask its borrowers to embrace a set of values known as the Sixteen Decisions. As a result, they have been encouraged to adopt positive social habits. One such habit is educating children by sending them to school. Today, almost all borrowers have their school-age children enrolled in regular classes. This one decision, in turn, helps bring about social change, and educate the next generation.

There is no legal instrument (no written contract) between the bank and its borrowers; the system works based on trust. In what has been termed solidarity lending, a small group from the same village is required to vouch for the borrower. If the loan cannot be repaid, no one is required to ante up the balance; however, access to new funds is now cut off. To supplement the lending, the bank also requires the borrowing members to save very small amounts regularly in a number of funds like emergency fund, group fund, and so forth. These savings help serve as an insurance against contingencies.

Another feature of the bank is that it is owned by the borrowers. Of the total equity, they own 94%, and the remaining 6% is owned by the Government of Bangladesh. It has grown significantly from its humble origins. As of October, 2007, the total borrowers numbered 7.34 million, and 97% of those were women. Similar growth can be observed in the number of villages covered, and Grameen now has a staff of over 24,703 employees with 2,468 branches covering 80,257 villages, up from 43,681 villages covered in 2003. It has distributed $11.35 billion in loans out of which $10.11 billion has been repaid.[25]

The rest is history with micro-credit and social business lending all the rage around the world. There are still failures, but largely there are far more success stories as the World Bank's own economist points out. In 2010, two important things happened with the Bangladesh survey. Statistics showed that poverty had dropped significantly, and the numbers proving it were published at a record pace. Poverty dropped from 40% in 2005 to 31.5% in 2010. Economic growth, a broader micro credit system, and stronger social safety net likely also contributed to the drop.[26]

Another example of taking an alternate world view is the story of Bob Harris whom I mentioned earlier. Bob had one of those jobs that on the surface that seemed to be ideal: traveling to the world's most elegant destinations on a special assignment for Forbes magazine. But the dream slowly faded as Bob's internal compass was moving his heart to the plight of the very poor that existed in the parallel universe adjacent to these lavish enclaves. Bob chose to give his entire $25,000 earnings from his work to Kiva. Kiva operates in a similar fashion as Grameen by allowing borrowers from around the world to access Bob's funds.   These are small business loans, helping a man in Paraguay, for example, expand his mosquito repellent wristband inventory or giving a palm tree climber in Cambodia the opportunity to increase his palm wine production.

One thing this approach doesn't do necessarily is change the hearts and minds of the ultra rich. Nevertheless, even in their circles where self interest rules, they are finding that sprinkling a few bucks among those poor folks creates massive new market opportunities for the goods and services they already control. Yes, it is true that micro credit opens up the possibility of another avenue of exploitation, but it also offers the potential for significant percentages of folks to lift themselves out of their circumstances.

Like intentional communities, co-ops, and employee owned businesses, these alternative lending enterprises provide us with many opportunities to visualize how individual initiatives can coalesce our collective consciences for the betterment of all. It is interesting to note that both

Marx and Yunus were economists, but the outcomes of their theories have had radically different consequences. Marx emphasized a radical restructuring of society by placing great value on everyone being assimilated, much like the villainous Borg of Star Trek fame modus operandi. Yunus' approach highlights individual initiative, allowing each person to contribute his or her creative capacity while maintaining a strong sense of self-worth. In fact, one of the criticisms of communities like the Harmonites and even the Bruderhof of today is that they are overly reliant on sameness in order to maintain their identity.

By changing our perspective, affirmative economic initiatives allow us to view solutions through the lens of those afflicted by it; therefore, it creates opportunities for them to develop and participate in solutions. I really don't sense it's a theological issue, yet we have made it one throughout the centuries. Gutierrez may disagree, but I simply don't believe that the role of the very poor in the grand scheme of life is to provide a redemptive platform for those in better circumstances. This point of view reinforces, however unintentional, a community that ultimately still remains divided into the haves and have-nots. Again, who would have thought if you just treated these folks like everyone else they might act like everyone else.

Given these circumstances, theologians, regardless of denominational persuasion, would best serve the poor by focusing their energies on the hearts and minds of those who create the culture that allows poverty to exist. That focus would mean uprooting the nullity of their efforts by more forcibly holding their flock to the importance of a living wage for those they might employ, as Tolstoy so ardently advocated and for which he was ultimately excommunicated.

Let us remember too, that beyond poverty lies destitution. For a billion or so of our brothers and sisters, this is a way of life where talk of salvation in these terms is rather minimal. However, if I were able to arrange a photo shoot with any of the aforementioned billionaires and an impoverished soul from the Democratic Republic of the Congo, standing side by side, who do you think in your heart of hearts is in need of life support? Is it the one who has nothing and cries out, "Why?", or the one who has everything and sheds not a tear?

---

[22] Tax Justice Network, Price of Offshore Revisited: Press Release 19th July 2012

[23] http://en.wikipedia.org/wiki/Wealth_and_religion#cite_note-17

[24] 2012 Human Development Report, United Nations

[25] http://en.wikipedia.org/wiki/Grameen_Bank

[26] A Win-Win in Bangladesh, Q&A with Nobuo Yoshida, Senior Economist at the World Bank, Dec. 1, 2011

CHAPTER 9

COMMOM SANDS

Hmm, this beach doesn't look the same as last year. There must have been some terrible storms down here this past winter. Oh, and look at those houses about to be retrieved by nature before their owners had intended. No Trespassing signs might deter a beachcomber, but the ocean takes its cue from an authority of a higher order than mortals.

We are walking along Chatham Lighthouse Beach, which sits below the watchful gaze of Chatham Light, an active lighthouse at the Coast Guard Station that aids in the navigation of Chatham Waters. Any number of multigenerational family members and friends might be included in this annual pilgrimage to take in the soothing elixir of this slice of paradise.

Neither the Monomoy peoples who lived here long ago nor most Americans of today, for that matter, can afford to reside here. What has been given freely by the Creator will now set you back over $1.2 million dollars if you want to maintain a residence, the average price of a home here in 2012.

Nevertheless, we can thank the Romans for originating the concept of a Public Trust Doctrine that allows mere plebeians to meander along the beach although we don't own it. Is this another entitlement for the masses restraining minority control? Works well, don't you think? Perhaps we might think of other opportunities where we might apply this enlightened approach to the public. The last time I checked "the public" encompasses all of us.

I digress again, for my thinking days are over, and I have no need to gaze out over the horizon. Or maybe I do…

CHAPTER 10

WHERE IS PEACE?

Not long ago, I was at the bedside of a ninety-seven year old relative. Although almost around the clock vigils were kept, no one was there when she passed from us. However, a few family members were first to see her and after dialoging with the nurses who had last checked in around noon, we were able to ferret out that she had died within the hour of our coming.

Although she carried her own personal travails, I was fortunate when in her presence to remember a person full of wisdom, able to identify edible mushrooms and a variety of birds on her walks through the yard. In other words, she exemplified a peaceful countenance to be in the company of. I struggled as I saw that her life ebbed away opposite the way she lived. Among other ails, what finally tipped the scales for her was liver cancer. As with many ways to die, this disease is extremely painful and her moments of awareness for her last months were agonizing calls to "go home" until the administered morphine allowed her to rest. Even asleep though, you could see she was not at peace. We are then left with those lingering words: "May She Rest in Peace." At this point, the spiritual sages must acknowledge that no one really knows what nurtures peace while living, so if you are one to believe in the afterlife, your solace might be found there.

The salvific value of eradicating poverty may or may not be the all encompassing elixir that heals our internal wounds. Defining "peace" has captured the imagination of philosophers, theologians, mystics and poets for eons. For an encyclopedic definition of "peace", I refer you to Wikipedia[27]. Given the accumulated wealth of knowledge on this topic, ask yourself, "How many folks do you know or have come across in your lifetime that you would describe as being at peace?

---

[27]http://en.wikipedia.org/wiki/Peace

CHAPTER 11

THE END

O ur lives have a finite span yet we live in an infinite universe. Perhaps salvation, noting we have a limited understanding of our nature, represents a quest to connect with this infinite source of our existence. Many have posited this theory in one form or another. I have wondered what it would be like to be walking the streets of Rome, pondering the rumor that another senator is now a Christian. Or what would motivate a Jew to depart from sound orthodoxy to consider the words from another Jew as providing a worthwhile alternate path to follow?

Jesus ben Sira declared, "Do not forget, there is no coming back," referencing a theological period where the idea of Sheol prevailed amongst many Jews. Sheol represented a religionless, Godless place where inhabitants inherited a diminished, joyless subsistence into a land of darkness that they entered through the grave.[28] This disconnected approach does not set well with most of us, thereby propelling us to consider a vivid afterlife, in one form or another, as a preferred way of viewing what lies beyond for us.

In 2013, Italian archaeologists claim to have uncovered in southwestern Turkey the gateway to Hades, the netherworld from classical Greek mythology. A cave in the ancient Phrygian city of Hierapolis, now Pamukkale, was once the site of pagan rituals where, according to the experts, priests sacrificed bulls to the god of the underworld, Hades (known as Pluto to the Romans).

"People could watch the sacred rites from these steps, but they could not get to the area near the opening. Only the priests could stand in front of the portal," indicated excavation leader Francesco D'Andria, professor of classic archaeology at the University of Salento. Among ancient ruins, they found a temple, a pool, and some steps above the cave, all of which corresponded to descriptions of the gateway from ancient texts. They also found columns with inscriptions to Hades and Persephone (Kore to the Romans), queen of the underworld.

The portal, known as Plutonium or Pluto's Gate, has long been noted for its lethal vapors and noxious odors. Pilgrims used to expose birds to the once-mysterious emanations to test the cave's deadliness. "This space is full of a vapor so misty and dense that one can scarcely see the ground. Any animal that passes inside meets instant death," wrote Strabo, a Greek geographer and historian (64 B.C. to about A.D. 24). Modern science reveals this mysterious presence to be merely carbon dioxide. "We could see the cave's lethal properties during the excavation," said D'Andria. "Several birds died as they tried to get close to the warm opening, instantly killed by the carbon dioxide fumes." These fumes would also induce spiritual visions for the priests. Simply put, they got high.

Christians destroyed Plutonium during the sixth century, and earthquakes finished off most of what was left. Now

D'Andria and his team are working on reconstructing the historic site digitally.[29]

Staggering amounts of time and talent have been devoted to deciphering the whys and wherefores of life after our physical death. I don't believe I have much to add to this body of knowledge. If we go back to my original premise that elegant solutions abound in the universe, it may be the simple desire to live on in spirit with our Creator in the world beyond. Like the intangible nature of love, we can only hope this idea is true. Moreover, just as it is on our earthly journeys, it is a comforting elixir to know that it might be. I do sense that is why so many folks in Rome, Jerusalem, and the surrounding countryside found Christianity appealing. Among many possibilities for this strong interest has to be the fact that it offered an antidote to that nagging anxiety they and we experience if we feel our lives have no greater calling than the ho-hum drum of daily existence. We certainly didn't and don't want to end up like Sisyphus, condemned to pushing up that boulder only to find it rolling back for him to do it again for all eternity. I think the Greeks, for the masterful legacy they left the universe depicted in their mythological writings, at the same time had a good handle on the drudgery we could concoct for ourselves in reality. This insight also might explain our struggle to seek alternatives to this misery at any or all costs.

It is interesting to note that one might be inspired by the anxiety of living in Hades while alive, or by contemplating what lies beyond our earthly existence. Following the path where the insights I've mentioned thus far have led, I believe what we seek is to be found in how we alter our lives in the here and now. A rose does not withhold the promise of its scent until we pass away but offers its gift to anyone who can appreciate it. The next few chapters explore the varied paths of some of the folks that have trod before us, preparing the ground for those of us on the way as they sought redemption from the plight of Sisyphus.

---

[28] The Resurrection, p6, Geza Vermes

[29] http://www.nydailynews.com/news/world/gateway-hades-
uncovered-turkey-archaeologists-article-
1.1307747#ixzz2Pe9z1yzc

CHAPTER 12

PEACE LATTE'

Imagine for a moment that you are whiling away a pleasant afternoon at the Salvation Cafe. It is rumored that it is frequented by a veritable who's who of masters, sages, and guru's from all over the world. There's Imam al-Bukhaari chatting with St. Augustine. Beyond them, you spot Maharishi Mahesh Yogi, Julian of Norwich, and Rabbi Yitzhak Saggi Nehor, also known as Isaac the Blind in quiet conversation. You also thought you spied Thomas Merton with Lao Tzu and Táhirih pulling in the parking lot behind you. You are hoping to be the benefice of the mystical air that permeates this sacred watering hole.

You have to admit that sometimes you eavesdrop on the conversations in hope of gaining the inside track on the ideal, perfect path to a sense of well being and peace. At times, you are rather mystified by the conversations. Rather than sage dialogue, it mostly centers on what you would term chitchat covering the rather rogue ways that led them to their exalted status. There is an air of confidence among these folks as exuded by any successful group whether it is in this heady game of offering insightful wisdom, playing hoops in the

NBA, or a gathering of CEO's on the golf course. However, you have noted a tinge of anxiety among this eclectic gathering, lest the masses sort out their storied past isn't all that different from their own perilous lives.

Quintus Aurelius Symmachus, consul of Rome in 391 A.D., appears still somewhat miffed when he makes an appearance with his entourage. In fact, his drink of choice, a quad espresso does nothing but exacerbate the situation. This gifted orator, statesman, and immensely wealthy aristocrat sensed his star was waning back then when he attempted to defend the status quo from the ensuing onslaught of Christianity. In fact, when filling the role as Prefect in 384 A.D., he wrote a now famous memorial to defend the traditional Roman perspective on theology.

Symmachus addressed it in the name of the Senate, nominally to the three Emperors- Valentinian, Theodosius, and Arcadius- though really to the first of these alone, who was sole Emperor of the West. The memorial sets forth a request that the old religion should be restored and the Altar of Victory again erected in the Senate House so that the ancient customs might be observed. The example of the late emperors should be followed in what they maintained, not in what they did away with. The treasury would suffer no loss, while it is unjust that the Vestal Virgins and priests should be deprived of ancient legacies, a sacrilege which the gods punished by a famine. The memorial is drawn up with consummate skill, both in what is brought forward and in what is left unsaid.[30]

In part, it reads, "We ask, then, for peace for the gods of our fathers and of our country. It is just that all worship should be considered as one. We look on the same stars, the sky is common, and the same world surrounds us. What difference does it make by what pains each seeks the truth? We cannot attain to so great a secret by one road; but this discussion is rather for persons at ease, we offer now prayers, not conflict."[31]

Symmachus was to learn firsthand that the Public Trust Doctrine ideal did not flow over to matters of theology, for many of his colleagues were converting to what then would be seen as heretical Christianity. As a side note, some things have loosened a bit these days, for he is always seen commiserating with the Vestal Virgins. The baristas fear this lot, for they can be quite demanding, meting out severe verbal abuse if the froth in the cappuccinos is not stiff, something that can be achieved only when appropriately chilled crucibles are used to steam the milk.

The Vestal Virgins, now a footnote in history having been officially abandoned in 394 A.D., had power and respect well beyond what we are led to believe in some quarters as ever existing in theological circles. Their positions carried considerable privilege as well as responsibility. At one point, they interceded on behalf of Julius Caesar, gaining him pardon after he was proscribed as an enemy of the state. Attempting to harm them was punishable by death; conversely, anyone touched or seen by a Vestal on their way to execution would be pardoned. The Vestals were freed of the usual social obligations to marry and bear children and took a vow of chastity in order to devote themselves to the study and correct observance of state rituals that were off limits to the male colleges of priests.

Given this backdrop to set the stage, let's take a closer look at some other personages we might run into if we stopped in to the café for our favorite "Peace Latte."

---

[30] Translation from Medieval Sourcebook: Ambrose Dispute with Symmachus, Introduction, Fordham University

[31] Translation from Medieval Sourcebook: Ambrose Dispute with Symmachus, section 415, Fordham University

CHAPTER 13

AT THE TABLE

SAINT AUGUSTINE

I consider the writings of St. Augustine to be some of the most insightful into our natures, certainly my own. Anyone who reconsiders his or hers own wisdom based on the continuum of human experience rates highly in my book. His station in life rose because of family connections, sheer intelligence, and his commanding presence in public forums. I have come to believe that the pinnacle of "making the sale" is found in ministry, leaving Zig Ziglar and the likes in the dust.

Over time, St. Augustine used his formidable skills endlessly rehabilitating himself from his many flaws. He was obviously "self-aware," and from an early age he could not hide his actions behind the smoke screen of "I was unaware of what I was doing." His life pretty much visited all the vices. As but one example, he had a live-in concubine of several years from which a child Adeodatus (Godsend) was born. He later sent the mother away as his star was rising. He would now need a compatible wife to match or enhance his station. A marriage suitably arranged by his mother Monnica. Later in life, he penned *What is Good in Marriage* that aptly crucifies his own behavior. It is interesting to note that this seriously flawed human ultimately became a Father of the Catholic Church. This paradox makes sense as his developing wisdom and the forming of authentic Church dogma were coming into complete alignment.

Peace, however, remained an elusive commodity for him. He was a tireless seeker, never satisfied. Like Aeneas, the hero of his favorite poem, he sailed toward ever-receding shores (Aeneid, 6.61). Impatient with all preceding formulations, even his own, he was drawn to and baffled by mystery: "Since it is God we are speaking of, you do not understand it. If you could understand it, it would not be God." (Sermons 117.5) We seek one mystery, God, with another mystery, ourselves.[32]

Even with his impressive life and grasp of the human condition, his last years were spent in a deeply anguished state. In his mid-seventies, the aging Augustine had the comfort, which had often been a trial, of living with a chosen band of brothers in his monastery. His discipline aimed at amity, and he threatened to leave the table if any monk ignored the verse he had cut into its wood:

Who gnaws with envy those who are away

May not bite food or at this table stay

When his last illness felled him, he asked the brothers to leave him alone in his cell, and the one who took him food found him weeping. He had asked that large-lettered copies of the penitential psalms be fixed to his cell's walls for him to go over and over, lamenting sins-not we may be sure, the long-ago sins of his youth. He tells us in book 10 of The Testimony (Confessions) that his life as a bishop was one of sin.[33]

My humble opinion is that Augustine could not grasp what his most insightful nature brought to light, and his only defense became his outlook. I sense that he felt himself a failure in that grace had not endowed him with perfection in both his outward and inner being. He had already solved our mysterious existence but never came to terms with what that knowledge implies. This reality may have required him to alter his outlook as he had done earlier in his life, opening the door to accept how grace makes its presence known. His writings certainly help me in that regard.

BUDDHA

Gautama Buddha had at least two similarities with St. Augustine if the historical record is reasonably accurate. I make this claim because much of what we know about Augustine was captured in the approximately five million words put down in writing in his own hand or by his scribes. What we know about Buddha was not captured in writing until about four hundred years after his death. I don't know about you, but sometimes what I recollect about what might have happened to me only a few weeks ago may be adequately embellished to suit my point of view.

At any rate, the first comparison is that Buddha did have a change of heart on his path to Nirvana and found The Middle Way offered a better approach to attaining it than the strict asceticism of his earlier years. The second similarity is that both left a spouse (married in this case) and a son behind in seeking their respective path to peace. Although, to his credit, some accounts indicate reconciliation occurred, and his son Rahula became a monk. Other accounts differ widely with one indicating that Rahula was not born naturally but by apparition. The biographical accounts are exceedingly sketchy for a man who lived approximately eighty years. As I indicated earlier, theologians of all stripes have taken advantage of this factual void to paint a mosaic to suit their needs. Very simply, the essence of Buddhist thought is to understand the profound impact suffering has on our lives. The Four Noble Truths outline the causes of suffering and the Eightfold Path presents a cure.

Essentially, Buddha taught that suffering was caused by greed and ignorance. This teaching is problematic, at least for me. It exemplifies a top down approach apparent in so much theological discourse for the point of view is from one who suffers from material wealth. This notion makes sense given Buddha's background but it really doesn't include the mass of humanity who, as Tolstoy so aptly portrayed, suffers from endless toil caused by much that is out of their control.

Both Hinduism and Buddhism have distilled our understanding of the human condition through stunning poetic verse and beautiful scripture. Again, I simply ask you to look at the results to date if you know of anyone to have even come close to eliminating suffering in their own lives by following these tenets. We may be able to come to terms with our state of mind and in this regard, the Eightfold Path can be quite helpful. Additionally, for many spiritual masters, the renouncing of material wealth is a pathway to enlightenment.

A friend of mine made an insightful observation in that this choice still represents an element of control whereby they are making a decision that many do not have. Don't you agree that it would be a rather novel idea for someone to renounce poverty to become an abbot, prince, or wealthy benefactor?

At his death, the Buddha is famously believed to have told his disciples to follow no leader. He also rejected the infallibility of accepted scripture: "Teachings should not be accepted unless they are borne out by our experience." I think this advice is one of the more profound aspects of his wisdom and certainly the most difficult for his devotees actually to live by as evidenced by the myriad of scholars who endlessly debate what can actually be attributed to his life. I think Buddha would smile at this conundrum. Perhaps the following story says it all.

Once, a very old king went to see a hermit who lived in a bird's nest in the top of a tree, "What is the most important Buddhist teaching?" the king asked.

The hermit answered, "Do no evil, do only good. Purify your heart."

The king had expected to hear a very long explanation. He protested, "But even a five-year old child can understand that!"

"Yes," replied the wise sage, "but even an 80-year-old man cannot do it."

It is exceedingly difficult to understand what Buddha's actual thoughts might have been as he navigated life. As I mentioned earlier, one can make a story to fit the situation. Some will ardently believe it; others will spend a lifetime disputing it. I try to use Buddha's approach in analyzing Buddhist thought to discern what is most likely true. First, he did not consider himself to be a deity and was only made so long after he was gone. This is important for he felt anyone could find enlightenment. This insight was a definite break from Hinduism.

The Autobiography of a Tibetan Monk by Palden Gyatso is the story of endless Tibetan suffering at the hands of the Chinese. Although a few like Palden lived to tell their stories, many did not. I don't believe he survived by practicing the Eightfold Path. It was more his sheer will, determination, hope, and luck than any ability to end suffering on his part or for any of his Tibetan brothers and sisters. It would be interesting to note what Gautama and Palden would say to each other should they ever meet at the Salvation Café.

ANGELA OF FOLIGNO

Angela of Foligno, an Italian born circa 1248 A.D., is now lauded as one of our great medieval mystics although much is not known about her except what is revealed in two works, *Memoriale* and *Instructiones*. You would be in luck to find two scholars who actually agree on the details of her life but that is not surprising. Here is what I found that seems to be the most authoritative compendium of a few basic facts.

Angela da Foligno was born either in 1248 A.D. or 1249 A.D. and died in 1309 A.D. Capable of reading but unable to write, most likely between 1292 A.D. and 1296 A.D., she dictated her spiritual experiences to Fra Arnaldo, a Franciscan brother. Although no doubt can be raised about the identity of Angela da Foligno, the name of Angela never appears in the text: she is always referred to as the *fidelis Christi*. While the fidelis Christi related her experiences in the vernacular of her native Umbria, the Franciscan scribe--according to his written statement in Il libro--wrote in her presence and translated her words into Latin. This first redazione of Angela's mystical experiences was then presented to the ecclesiastical authorities and to a group of Franciscan theologians for their approval. This official approval or testificatio, marks the beginning of what is currently called the second redazione.

The original transcription of Angela's experiences is lost, and the reconstruction of the critical text has been most difficult. The tradition of Angela's writings has been divided into no fewer than eight families with twenty-nine manuscripts. The oldest manuscript, which is in Assisi, is a copy of an exemplar of another exemplar, being thus three times removed from the original text. The title assumes no fewer than six different appellations in the tradition of the manuscripts and in printed editions and to call it Memoriale is only a conjecture. In fact, one might even submit that the book has no title. Thus, in the case of Angela da Foligno's Memoriale, the mystic to whom the writing is attributed finds herself somewhat removed from her own life account because she was not involved directly in the physical act of writing. Furthermore, the issue of authorship becomes further complicated because of the peculiar nature of mystical experiences described first through the spoken word and second through the written word by means of a scribe.[34]

Angela's appeal seemed to lie in her absolute belief in her personal relationship with Christ. This powerful notion draws us near to folks having insight on how best we conduct our lives. It adds considerable credibility if we believe the messenger is in communication with our God. Angela lived not many years removed from the time of Assisi and drew much from his experiences in shaping her own salvation. I always struggle with this notion as being quite egotistical to believe that God would choose me for special treatment.

Nevertheless, this caution is quite often ignored, and we have many, many folks up to the present day who develop quite a following after experiencing personal revelations from their Creator. This process often goes along with physically separating oneself from family ties. Angela also had a spouse and children and was not terribly upset when they died off, freeing her to do God's work.

"In that time and by God's will there died my mother, who was a great hindrance unto me in following the way of God; my husband died likewise, and in a short time there also died all of my children. And because I had commenced to follow the aforesaid way and had prayed God that He would rid me of them, I had great consolation of their deaths, albeit I did also feel some grief."[35]

Depending on their point of view, we can learn much about our human condition by the way various scholars treat this passage. I suspect it is reasonably close to the truth. Once again, like Assisi, the Ten Commandments proved no obstacle to the esteemed place she finds herself in today with congresses, film, and stage productions depicting her life and a renewed attempt to have her canonized as a saint.

I have spent much time thinking about how this scenario plays out in our everyday lives. There have been periods where I too have felt that the pressures and responsibilities of family were overwhelming, and it would be very appealing to withdraw into the religious life. I am not sure I have an answer to this dilemma. It just doesn't make sense that a path to enlightened wisdom is revealed when we sever our secular relationships in order to have a personal relationship with the Creator in order to be put on a path to salvation for oneself and others one might encounter in ministry. Historical records, however, bear out that often this circumstance is the case.

In practice, this condition has the potential to cast a shadow on "religious," and that portrayal is not my intention. I simply now view them, whether historically speaking or those I might encounter today, through the same lens as anyone else: mutual respect is earned and not divinely granted.

Whether or not Angela found peace and grace in her life is completely subject to conjecture. I've included her here as a stunning example of our propensity to see in the mirror of our lives exactly what we want to see reflected back to us. We can only hope that the redemptive strands of time will make us over in the same fashion.

MARJORY KEMPE

The Book of Marjory Kempe, like Augustine's Confessions, is an autobiographical account of her life. In attempting to understand what has been written about her, there is considerable psychobabble that creates a smoky haze over what she was thinking, for those thoughts were committed to the written word. Once again, chronicling the lives of mystics is big business. I think Margery would think it rather amusing that she created sustainable employment for so many folks up to the present day.

If we can peek through that haze and simply look at what is written, we might find a compelling story of one person's life's journey, not unlike ours in the 21st century, making allowances for the fact that it was written in the Middle Ages. One aspect of her life is that she did not fit into that category that befits most of us leading lives of quiet desperation. She acted out, sometimes vociferously, in the public arena what many of us carry in our hearts. In other words, she made a scene at various locales causing consternation among the many people she encountered. At one point, she was even questioned for possible heretical behavior.

Ultimately, she seems to come to terms with her life better than most lives of the mystics that are chronicled, yet considerable turmoil was always around the corner. She was unique in that, although now considered a great mystic, at the end of her life she had not completely abandoned her family as it seems is the criteria for so many who follow a spiritual calling. She did have fourteen children and I have no idea what happened to all of them but at least one is mentioned in her book with which she maintained a relationship. She helped him through a difficult period in his own life. Her compelling visions moved her to travel frequently for long periods. Initially, her husband was her companion, but eventual they lived separate lives for many years; however, when he fell and became disabled, she took him in and cared for him. Although she had this passionate and sometimes controversial relationship with Christ, it was not to the complete exclusion of those from her temporal past.

THOMAS MERTON

As with Augustine, we have been endowed with a prolific output of the writings of Thomas Merton. There is a good mix of personal diaries, memoirs, and topical material to give us a good sense of who he really was. He has provided a generation of scholars much material to pore over for dissertations, symposiums, and classroom curricula. I cannot add much to the insights already opined. For me, I can only say that his writings give us a very personal view of the "quintessential" journey. His exploration of spirituality left no stone unturned and we are right there with him as he peeks under each one. In many ways, he represented a contemporary version of the mortification process prevalent in the Middle Ages.

Many of Merton's adherents indicate that he had come full circle by the time he reached the end of his tragically shortened life, but I am doubtful. In his Asian Journals, it is apparent that his emotional reach was as far flung as ever. He wrote of settling in Alaska upon his return in hopes that it might provide the setting that proved so elusive for him. Sometimes, I think his intellectual prowess ultimately proved an obstacle to finding the proverbial Holy Grail hidden beneath one of those rocks. His exquisite analysis always just fell short of that simple elegant solution he was seeking to his own salvation. For that effort, I am grateful, as he helped me see that words may not always lead where we hope they might. Unfortunately, only in Hollywood can we write scripts of lives as we would think they ought to be portrayed.

If I were penning Merton's story, it might end with me writing to Abbot Flavian Burns at Gethsemani, indicating that his sojourn in Bangkok would be his last. He would lay down his pen upon his return to Kentucky, spending his days tending the soil with many of the impoverished souls who eked out a living in the surrounding hills of their Abbey. "We have much to learn from each other."

RICHARD WURMBRAND

Some personal journeys can lead to unlikely outcomes. At times, the puzzling circumstances we as humans find ourselves in can serve as counterweights to the dark side of our existence. We may never overcome the many tragedies that befall us, and perhaps that is the insight we are to glean from the seemingly unfair circumstances that taunt us in our daily lives.

Richard Wurmbrand's life is one such story. Of Jewish heritage, he became an Anglican and then Lutheran minister. With such an unlikely background, it's not surprising that he found himself in hot water with Communist authorities after they seized power in Romania in 1945.

Richard managed to survive through years of imprisonment and torture at the hands of his captors by writing and preaching sermons to his flock. Remarkably, the sermons were only "written" in his head, and the flock was imaginary. After being ransomed from his second imprisonment, he and his wife Sabina landed in America. He then continued his ministry, which eventually became the VOM or "Voice of the Martyr" which exists to this very day.

His story is compelling on many levels. One example is that he wasn't imprisoned because he had a gun in his hand ready to shoot at the invaders. His ammunition was of a different caliber, for it may impact your being without as much as a scratch to the body. History has taught us that this is far more dangerous than an AK-47 in the hands of the right person. Richard aptly filled this role. His entire ministry today centers on helping folks who find themselves persecuted for their Christian beliefs. I do not believe it advocates for any other belief system, but whatever the case, the fact that this organization exists at all is a telling reminder of the role faith journeys have led and continue to lead to bloody conflicts around the world. Conflicts arise across the entire spectrum of sacred and secular adherents around the globe.

Like Palden Gyatso, Richard and his cell mates suffered mightily at the hands of totalitarian Communist regimes, yet both he and Palden survived. To me, they represented the epitome of the titanic struggle between free will and its suppression. Their captors could have easily put a bullet in their heads, game over. But the purpose of the war wasn't to defeat but to control, and it becomes more like a game of chess where mental prowess reigns. My all time favorite Star Trek episodes involved the "Borg." "Resistance is futile" and "You will be assimilated" were a few of the classic taunts spoken to undermine the will of the invaded species. To me, they represented creative genius on the part of script writers for succinctly capturing the essence of our human struggle. The only difference is that they portrayed the Borg as coming from another part of the universe rather than as a metaphor for what is already with us.

Those attracted to power, whether pastoral or temporal, fully understand that if you control the mind, you own the body and soul. Many individuals were martyred for not submitting to the will of an overwhelming adversary. Joan of Arc, Thomas More, Guru Arjun Dev, and Swami Lakshmanananda are but a few who did not survive. Interestingly, there is considerable evidence indicating that Christian evangelicals aligned with Communist Maoists assassinated the Swami after seven previous failed attempts.

For me, the takeaway on Richards' legacy is that it remains glaringly obvious that The Public Trust doctrine mentioned earlier would be a good idea for theologians to embrace. Perhaps they could work with Google to develop a "Theologically Speaking" app to eliminate doctrinal divides acting somewhat like a USB port that, regardless of what anyone communicated, would be instantly recognized by the reader as doctrinally correct. Like a grain of sand, we would retain our individual notions of salvation and might soon realize we walk on the same beach in more ways than we thought.

SOARING EAGLE

In my observations, the symbiosis between those who feel called to missionary work in one form or another and those that benefit from their efforts is quite striking. Once again, the reason for selecting these particular individuals to write about as opposed to any other is beyond me. One thread is that, ultimately, the line between who is offering salvation and who is receiving it becomes quite blurred as one follows the intricacies of their life stories.

This man would rank high on the who's who list of missionaries. A master fundraiser, a visionary behind the building of schools, churches, businesses, retirement, and recreational facilities only scratches the surface of his legacy. He was also an alcoholic, had an adopted Cheyenne daughter, married a wife by proxy, was accused of abuse, piloted planes, and delivered babies. Again, an abbreviated list, and oh, I almost forgot, an ordained priest and brother of the Capuchin order, Father Emmett Hoffmann was born in 1926 and passed to the "Maheo," the Creator God of the Northern Cheyenne in 2013.

Reading of his early assessment of religious experience is refreshing for his candor in describing life behind its well cultivated façade. "If it had been real, I would have followed the rules, but the whole Catholic seminary system was a game. You played their game, and you were okay. You were either a sinner or a 'scroop,' a scrupulous religious person. I didn't go for the 'Holier than Thou' mentality. But whatever they wanted, I gave it to them."[36]

"He felt the so-called "vow of poverty" was a sham. It looked to him like the poverty vow meant living in a palatial mansion and having all his needs met. The Novitiate was a time-out, when a man learned about religious life, but for Emmett, living in a beautiful home like Huntington was not living in poverty-it was pure luxury compared to the farm."[37]

Ultimately, he did experience extreme poverty, both physical and mental, during his tenure among the Northern Cheyenne. When he arrived in Montana in July 1954, he was shocked by the impoverished living conditions, the forgotten victims of neglect by the U. S. Government. They were drinking from contaminated wells and suffering from one of the highest TB rates in the nation. Malnourished families crowded into thin wall tents and old log cabins in temperatures of 40 degrees below zero.

In the coming years, Father's superiors tried to transfer him to other parish posts, as was the custom, but the Cheyenne gathered numerous signed petitions to block his placement elsewhere. In an effort to show how serious the Cheyenne were to keep Father Emmett with them, they made him an Honorary Chief of the Northern Cheyenne Council of 44, one of only two white men in history to attain that honor. At that time, he was given the moniker "Soaring Eagle."

Under Father Emmett's direction, St. Labre Indian School went from a few condemned buildings with less than 100 students to one of the finest, modern, Indian schools in the nation with an enrollment of 700 students in three schools.

After a Sabbatical in 1981, Father Emmett helped to construct St. Bernard's Church in Billings. Then he returned to St. Labre to build the Soaring Eagle Center, a 52,000 square foot facility containing an auditorium with 419 seats, a full basketball court, 2 practice courts, an indoor track, racquetball courts, a weight room, a sauna, and an Olympic-sized swimming pool.

But my focus here in retelling a bit of his story is how transformative his time with a people in need of much help was for him. Indeed, it took a lifetime, but any salvation he found on this earth was rendered as a gift from those he came to save. This gruff, egotistical juggernaut who provided so much in the way of material gains to this impoverished land and its people was to learn, almost by osmosis, that in a spiritual sense, he had so much more to learn from them about living through the peaks and valleys of his personal life. He was able to draw strength, insight, and a measure of peace by learning from those whose daily survival was at risk. Their way of life, as practiced in their traditions, gave them hope to sustain themselves through lives riddled with strife.

As with the rest of humanity, the Cheyenne continue to struggle with poverty, crime, and political machinations, pretty much a microcosm of what lies beyond tribal boundaries. President Richard Nixon, in his message to the Congress on July 8, 1970, said, "I am asking Congress to pass a new Concurrent Resolution which would expressly renounce, repudiate, and repeal the termination policy as expressed in HRC 108 of the 83rd Congress." This resolution would explicitly affirm the integrity and right to continued existence for all Indian Tribes and Alaska Native Governments, recognizing that cultural pluralism is a source of national strength.

Public Trust wins the day again, and if Emmett were still alive, he might simply chime in using that old familiar corporate slang, "It's a win-win situation."

Alias "La Sister"

I had not previously heard of Mary Clarke when I first came across the biography of Mother Antonia by Mary Jordon and Kevin Sullivan. In the twilight of her legacy, Mary is now achieving a similar status as Mother Theresa with extensive media coverage of her extraordinary life. In fact, if one were to write a fictional script based on her experiences, I would suspect that most would indicate that what was written could never happen. But there's always the adage that success breeds forgiveness and like Father Emmett, Mary Clarke was a powerful personage long before she took the habit as a nun, and this served her well in her ministry. As an older divorcee, Mother Antonia was banned by church rules from joining any religious order, so she went about her work on her own. In time, she founded an order for those in her situation: the Servants of the Eleventh Hour. Ultimately, in 2003, the community was formally accepted by the Bishops of Tijuana and San Diego.[38]

In the late 1970s, Mary Clarke, now called Mother Antonia, left her life as a wealthy, twice divorced mother of seven in Beverly Hills to live and work in one of Mexico's most notorious prisons, La Mesa State Penitentiary in Tijuana, historically one of Latin America's most violent. She lived in a ten by ten concrete room with a cot as her bed and with a Bible and Spanish dictionary nearby. When asked by guards and prisoners why she was there, she answered, "For the love of God and for the love of you all!" She began by tending to prisoners' immediate physical needs, but quickly moved beyond this to tackle the root of the problem: the Mexican justice system. She continued until her mid-eighties to minister to prisoners, prison guards, and their families.

A compelling insight into her life in later years comes from a talk she gave at a church, having recently returned from yet another prison riot. She was 82, the year was 2008, and she was still living in the prison.

On September 15, a riot broke out at the La Mesa penitentiary; at least four inmates died in the ensuing melee. Mother Antonia was not inside at the time. "I said, 'Let me go in.' 'I know I can do something to stop the violence.' But they wouldn't allow me in.... They were afraid for my safety. But the prisoners wouldn't have hurt me. I'm not afraid. When you love, you don't have anything to be afraid of. Love casts out fear, the Bible tells us, and I love the men there.... I can go into the cells and cellblocks, see the men, pray for them, and bring them hope."

"But", she added, "that doesn't mean I'm in accord with them. I'm going to show them what's wrong and try to calm something down that's evil and wrong. It just doesn't stop me from loving them." She lamented the loss of the prison's kitchen, laundry room, art room, classrooms, music room, library, and computer room — all burned in the riots. "Rage takes love completely out of your heart. Everything that was destroyed was for them, for the very men themselves."

The tragedy continued two days later on September 17. According to the San Diego Union-Tribune, "Female inmates began to riot just before 1 p.m. More than a dozen women climbed on top of the prison's building no. 7, where they are housed, and began to break lights and scream to a throng of people on the sidewalk outside. They shouted that they were being beaten and that there were dead and injured inmates inside. Rioting then spread to other buildings."

This time, Mother Antonia was inside. "They bolted my door. They were firing shots against the outside of my wall. They were firing to frighten everybody, making noise with guns, the helicopters overhead. I don't know how many bullets were shot over three and a half hours of shooting, but there were seventeen dead after this, and only two bodies have been claimed. The sisters, God bless them; bury the dead that are not claimed. But why? Mexican families always come to claim their dead. Why? Because they were deported. They didn't live in Tijuana. About 300,000 people were deported from the U.S. into Tijuana since 2006. What do you do when there are 300,000 people in a city without jobs, without credentials, without families? I'm hoping that the riot will move the government to take deported people and send them to their homes, all over Mexico. It's better than to have them live in rage and murder people...and murder themselves. Self-hate is terrible."

Mother Antonia's mention of political policy was born of personal events — the unclaimed bodies of the dead — and her talk hewed close to the personal and to the prosaic. She begged the congregation not to shame anybody. "It's a terrible thing to do to people. People will forget many things, but they do not forget being shamed." She called the tongue "a deadly weapon" and said that "the tongue caused this riot to start again. The men had calmed down, and the women were yelling, 'Help us!' and nothing was happening to them. Then the men broke through walls and started more fires, and pretty soon you had seventeen dead because of the tongue. The tongue destroys; it takes away hope.... Jesus said, 'Don't worry about your hand being dirty. Worry about the dirt that's on your heart; that speaks through your mouth.'"

She had some notion of what caused the women to cry out. "They've been victims of rape, of beatings, of pornography. Of being bought and sold. Of being treated like trash. They had a chance to explode themselves, to say, 'Now I'm going to be in control. Nobody's going to take me and do what they want with me.' So have pity on them."

This came in the midst of a cry against pornography: "Many good people, especially men, have become addicted to pornography with the Internet. Porn is satanic; it's evil. It enters the brain and it doesn't leave. The devil never sleeps. Evil doesn't sleep. But neither does good, and good is much more powerful than evil."

Against all this, she spoke of love. "Love is patient. Love is kind. Those two things, patience and kindness. There are three ways to get to heaven. 'Be kind' is the first one." It was also the second and third. She urged her listeners to love. Listening to a gabby relative was "a holy hour." So was visiting the old and alone. "As long as you have to do something for somebody, you're blessed. Give thanks to God that you can do that." [39]

In her biography, Mother Antonia speaks freely about her anxieties over her lost marriages and not finding fulfillment in her professional life. Moving to her new life was the most difficult on her fifteen year old son who was still living with her at the time. But based on interviews, it seemed most family members felt that her calling was the thing to follow, and they have maintained relationships over the years. It must have been difficult though, in her private moments, to accept that like poverty, the conditions have not changed all that much with the aforementioned riots as an example. Like Fr. Hoffmann, she certainly experienced her own salvation from choosing a destitute situation and the folks she encountered in her ministry.

DENVER & RON

Many aspects of the autobiographies of Denver Moore and Ron Hall make for a best seller. Money, tragedy, triumph, and intrigue are but a few of the elements that make it so, but what I found most compelling is that their story is one of the few that explicitly explores the reciprocal needs of those that offer ministry and those that receive it. Their book, *Same Kind of Different as Me,* coauthored with Lynn Vincent, gives equal credence to the grace bestowed on Ron (art dealer) by his interaction with Denver (homeless man), hence, the title and the fact that the book was penned using both of their perspectives. The unlikely friendship that sprang up between Ron and Denver explores the many ways in which it was life saving for both men.

Denver Moore was born in rural Louisiana in 1937. He experienced a number of tragic events as a child, extreme poverty and the racism of that era. In 1966, he was sentenced to twenty years of hard labor in Angola Prison in Louisiana. When he was released in 1976 after serving ten years, he traveled to Fort Worth and spent the next twenty-two years homeless. He would occasionally ride the hobo trains around the U.S. He became an artist, public speaker, and volunteer for homeless causes, passing away in 2012.

Ron Hall was born in Texas in 1945 and was raised in Fort Worth, attending elementary and high school there. After graduating from Texas Christian University, he joined the Army. Upon completion of his military service, he worked as a salesperson for Campbell Soup. He married Deborah Short and returned to graduate school where he obtained an MBA and went to work as a municipal bond trader. However, he did not remain in this position but accidentally launched a successful career as an international art dealer and became a wealthy man.[40]

The three met when Ron and Debbie begin volunteering at a Fort Worth, Texas, homeless shelter and food kitchen. Denver, having lived a life on the streets, was generally wary of strangers and distrusting of those who say they just want to help, but Debbie was determined to get through to him. She saw something special there, and she encouraged Ron to forge a friendship with this seemingly unreachable man. Ironically, Ron was really no different than Denver, and it took quite some time for him to peel back the layers shrouding his well cultivated persona.

In fact, Denver, in spite of his past, had much to offer the relationship with his insightful wisdom. His last few lines in the book sum it up better than anything I could write: "I found out everybody's different—the same kind of different as me. We're all just regular folks walkin' down the road God done set in front of us. The truth about it is, whether we is rich or poor or something in between, this earth ain't no final restin' place. So in a way, we is all homeless—just workin' our way toward home."[41]

---

[32] Saint Augustine, p. xii, Garry Willis

[33] Saint Augustine, p.143, Garry Willis

[34]href="http://www.thefreelibrary.com/Angela+da+Foligno%27s+M emoriale%3A+the+male+scribe,+the+female+voice,+and...- a0143337397">Angela da Foligno's Memoriale: the male scribe, the female voice, and the other.</a>

[35] The Book of Divine Consolation of the Blessed Angela of Foglino, Tranlated from the Italian by Mary G. Steegmann, Chatto & Windus 1909

[36] Renegade Priest, p47, Renee Sansom Flood

[37] Renegade Priest, p48, Renee Sansom Flood

[38] Prison Angel, Mary Jordan & Kevin Sullivan, 2005

[39]Excerpt from San Diego Reader, Mother Antonia Speaks, Mathew Lickona, Sept.24th, 2008

[40] Catholic Library Association, www.cathla.org/ completed guides

[41] Denver Moore/Ron Hall, Same Kind of Different as Me, p235

CHAPTER 15

ENLIGHTENMENT 101

What insights, if any, might we glean from the vignettes portrayed in the previous chapter? First, as with all that have come before us, we are seekers. The life stories of folks that have risen to the top of the spirituality charts offer us hope that we might gain some of the wisdom for ourselves that they appear to have. "Beacons of Light" in what can often be the abysmal landscape of our human condition.

When I first meandered thru those "spiritual stacks" mentioned earlier, I began to purchase books written by some of the most prominent gurus of our time. I also nurtured a general interest in the origins of theology as it evolved out of philosophical perspectives. Over a period of roughly five years, both from what I was reading and my first hand endeavors with other like minded folks, I began to question if I felt any core changes in my being. Perhaps because I don't possess an encyclopedic memory, but the thousands upon thousands of "nuggets of wisdom" from the sages were simply dulling my senses rather than offering the promised enlightenment.

As a result, I began making some mid-course corrections to my Enlightenment 101 journey. I began to look for potentially good reads in the spiritual clearance racks at Half-Price Books, so my journey became one of "half-priced spirituality." That way, I reduced my risk, both emotionally and in the pocketbook, as I felt less obligated to force myself to read something that didn't merit the cover art.

A second insight accrued when I realized that many of the people we revere and expect to glean wisdom from often held many dark elements to their character, yet we have come to respect them for the various ways they sought a healing nature in their being. I hope these brief bios have helped you see that as they have helped me. If they found ways to accept their flawed nature and move beyond it, so can any of us.

The third insight is that the historical record of salvation handed down through the ages is the province of the rich, much like every other aspect of our human existence. I began asking of those around me, "Well, thank-God for the poor; what we would we do without them?" It became, at least for me, glaringly obvious that something is wrong if this scenario is one of the foundational pillars of salvation. Now, I didn't have the empirical facts to back this up, but it got to the point that regardless of what text I perused, I began to assume that the major theological characters came from privileged backgrounds. There exists the adage that history is written by the victors, and that seems to hold true for what has been handed down theologically over the centuries. It would also explain why there are so few "Denvers" in the historical record.

I came across an article while researching material for this book that actually does use statistical research to bear out what I intuitively came to feel. Rodney Stark provides a compelling story in work that he conducted on the social aspects of ascetic movements.

Most social scientists still agree with Marx that religion is rooted in the suffering of the poor, despite the fact that dozens of studies have found that class is, at most, barely related to religious belief and that the middle and upper classes dominate religious participation. These facts are eluded by the claim that it is intense religion, such as asceticism, that is the real "opium of the people." This essay presents data on a variety of ascetic movements, beginning as far back as the first Buddhist monks, which indicate that they were primarily vehicles for upper class piety. Then, the biographies of 483 ascetic, medieval Catholic saints (500-1500) are examined. These data reveal that they came primarily from the nobility.

The fundamental mechanism said to account for the piety of the poor is referred to as transvaluation of values-the capacity of religion to turn "worldly" values upside down. Hence, the have-nots redefine poverty as virtue and wealth as sinful, concluding that what they cannot have, they should not have, and that through these means "last shall be first, and the first last."

I incline to the view that the ascetic impulse is more prevalent among persons of privilege, sometimes reflecting guilt about having wealth, but more often stemming from the discovery that wealth is not fulfilling. Andrew Greeley pointed out that "it was only the nobility who had the time and opportunity to become saints" as the peasants were too busy trying to scratch out a living. Exactly! Hungry peasants are starving, not fasting. Deprivation is asceticism only when it is voluntary and that does tend to limit it to those with the privilege, even the burden, of choice. As Robert William Fogel explained, throughout history…freed of the need to work in order to satisfy their material needs, the rich have sought self realization.

He goes on to draw parallels to today's wealthy class, not aristocracy by any means, but still dominate in religious circles. The monks at San Francisco's celebrated Zen Center were overwhelmingly supported by wealthy families who provided them with regular checks or trust funds. Upon reflection, this was my own experience with many folks I encountered in the peace movement of the 60's.

He concludes; Thus, Marx might better have said, "religion is often the opium of the dissatisfied upper classes, the sigh of wealthy creatures depressed by materialism." But, of course, given his preoccupation with money, Marx couldn't conceive of such a thing.[42]

My personal experience only added to this paradoxical situation. If I entered a church in rags and seemingly disheveled but did not ask for help, it would be assumed I needed it and much would be offered. On the other hand, if I came in seemingly disheveled but well dressed and actually asked for help, most folks backed away or referred me to someone else. Try it yourself and see what happens.

I have been on both sides of this scenario. Once, I was on a self-directed weekend retreat. "Self-directed" implies no structure, so a few of us decided to walk to a small chapel nestled on a grassy knoll a couple of miles away from the main property. As we mingled just outside the entrance and enjoyed the tranquility of the place, a car raced up, and out stepped a person that fits this latter category. In a matter of moments, I found myself alone listening and in my own feeble way attempting to console this distraught individual. The situation eventually stabilized, and as we returned, the other folks commented that they felt badly for backing away and were glad I did not. I, on the other hand, don't know why I did the right thing at that particular moment when often I have not.

I am certain that Prozac and its variants find equal distribution among rich and poor. Poverty of soul does not discriminate, so this whole notion of how we have come to view salvation as moving linearly in one direction does not fit with the simple elegant solution theory I keep hoping to zero in on.

Perhaps, like a compass, this last insight helps us navigate beyond the façade of our motivations. We have seen that giving away all that one has is not necessarily a good barometer of the well-being of the giver. The desire to assuage guilt or a need to have a more meaningful existence can and often is independent of the outcome to the receiver of such largesse. I place guilt and ego on par with personal fulfillment as barriers that can easily mask the condition of our soul. In 626, Taizong, aided in his coup by Buddhist priests, crowned himself emperor of the Tang Dynasty, overthrowing his father and executing his brothers and untold adversaries. He later became known as a benevolent despot, for he began to cultivate his intellectual curiosity with the empire firmly in his grip. He built a 200,000 volume library and employed a myriad of intellectuals to feed his quest. His reach extended to theology, where it is said he explored the teachings of Christ through Bishop Aleben who had travelled 3000 miles across the Silk Road after being summoned to the imperial palace in Xian. Taizong ascribed the name "The Luminous Religion" to this new creed. In 1890, a Taoist monk named Wang Yuanlu discovered thousands of artifacts in caves high above the Silk Road called the cliffs of Dunhuang. Included were a unique set of eight scrolls later to be known as "The Jesus Sutras" which provided a written record of Aleben's teachings. At any rate, it is said that Taizong's trajectory was fueled with blood, but he possessed a charisma and personal magnetism attractive to the finest minds of his times. Nothing has changed over the millennia, as a listener to NPR will be quite often reminded that the programming is funded by benevolent XYZ Trust. The only difference is that the blood and sweat shed to build the robber baron fortunes of today comes from both the battlefield and the factory floor.

Conversely, being poor is not a free ticket to sanctity, allowing one to justify any actions of ill-will as being covered under the "umbrella policy" of one's station in life. In the streets of Calcutta where Mother Theresa worked there were stunning examples of impoverished individuals, when given food, would offer it to someone else in even greater need. At the same time, others would steal what they could even if it meant their family would continue to starve.

I can't help but sense that the answer lies in those grains of sand on "salvation beach". We are "homeless" until we recognize our equality before the Creator, capable of fabricating a magnificent beach we can all walk on. If only we believe it can be.

I do, what about you?

[42] Stark, Rodney: "Upper Class Asceticism: Social Origins of Ascetic Movements and Medieval Saints" in *Review of Religious Research*, no. 45, no. 1, September 2003, p. 5-19.

CHAPTER 16

VIBRATIONS

Vibes can be good or bad depending on the situation. We are using our intuitive sense when we say, "I feel good around her," thus defining the first state. If I lived near the epicenter of the tsunami that struck Japan a few years back, the vibes I experienced of impending doom are but one example of the latter.

The ones I'm feeling right now are those of a train rumbling down the valley. They remind me of an actual birthday wherein my gift was to experience a train ride on tracks and in cars restored by devotees of this rather luxurious way to navigate from point A to point B. Recreating that sense of time and place of an era gone by gave these folks much satisfaction, missionaries of a different calling. My wife, as befitting the first class passenger treatment that was part of the package, prepared a sumptuous feast for all to enjoy. It was a meal "to die for" as the saying goes. I can still taste the exquisite Black Forrest Cake that would rival any the bakers could make in that neck of the woods to be sure. That era faded away like the train on the tracks, which no longer operates because of legal liability hurdles, insurmountable compared to the daunting task of laying those meandering tracks in the first place.

The memory, however, lives on to stoke the flames of an extraordinary, ordinary life. Doesn't it feel like the train is still moving? I wonder where it's going. Hmm, but this cannot be; soon, I'll be hearing things.

CHAPTER 17

EGO-TRIPPED

Moving from where we are to where we might be is quite obviously terribly difficult, for if it were not, we would have been there by now. Botulinum is the most acutely toxic substance known, yet a derivative is used for the treatment of upper motor neuron syndrome, such as cerebral palsy, and for cosmetic applications under the savvy marketing moniker of Botox. In 2012, it was first reported that the venom of the Black Mamba, aside from being a lethal toxin, also carries a painkiller as powerful as morphine without the potentially harmful side effects. There are many examples of this duality of purpose in nature. The parallel for us is to think of our humility as the antidote to ego. The world is viewed differently when our egos are in check. There is no serum to inoculate ourselves against the ravages of an overactive ego. Over time, however, we can learn to bend our will to sublimate rather than fuel the appetite of our ferocious egos. The individuals outlined in previous chapters provide us with living proof that, to varying degrees, we are all capable of achieving this desired outcome.

It is my opinion that this idea represents one of the dominant threads of our earthly journeys. There is not a single instance of human interaction in my life where, upon reflection, my worst self can be traced back to not living up to this simple standard. When I find myself slipping into my unconscious self and am ready to spout off something derogatory about someone I have difficulty communicating with, I am always astonished if I can instead choose an alternative set of thoughts, something out of character, to bridge this gap and find it is warmly received. Try it yourself and see what happens.

I'll be honest; I quite often miss the mark, but like St. Augustine, I am self-aware, and the time between saying something foolish and realizing it is diminishing. It is an awareness that can be cultivated until doing the right thing becomes our nature rather than the default "human nature" used to explain our lower self. When we recognize this reality in all of our interactions, we begin to sense the redemptive spirit awakening in our being. It is the only way for a rich person to view a poor person as an equal and vice versa. It is the only way for an employer to view an employee or a government to view its citizens, for one culture to respect another. Like the composition of our salvation beach, one grain of sand, unique but of the same substance as all others.

There are many tools in our toolkit available for us to use in our everyday lives to drive the engine of personal transformation. One example I use myself is to remember "I am flawed; I am you" every time I interact with someone else. That ensures that my ego is suitably subdued so that I view the person as having as much to offer me as I to them. Am I capable of doing this all the time? Absolutely not, but like fine wine I can only hope I am improving with age.

Although there is no actual record, one of the many nuggets of wisdom attributed to St. Francis of Assisi is "Preach the gospel, and whenever necessary use words." In reality, I find this quite difficult as it so much easier to write, to speak, or to sing in elegant verse that helps us articulate what we know we should do but much, much harder to actually live it day in and day out. The honesty of Denver comes to mind as he never glossed over what he once was and knew full well he could be that person again. In fact, the dark side of his persona was always with him but it went into remission as he, unlike St. Augustine and so many others found that he could reach that "far shore," by letting his actions provide sustenance to those he encountered on his redemptive journey.

Can we diminish the impact of our ego to have negligible impact on our outlook or none at all? I would opine that it is wiser to nourish a healthy ego, for it is yet another of those human attributes with a duality of purpose. Many of the folks we've covered in this book would not have contributed to our greater good had they viewed their life as insignificant and meaningless. Like developing our will, cultivating a healthy ego takes time and effort. To negate one's ego entirely can actually drive us to despair, quite the opposite of hope.

A good example would be to look at the lives of two folks who share a last name but were not related, Krishnamurti. U.G. Krishnamurti felt he had a major transformative event around the age of 49 that he characterized as a death experience giving birth to what he termed a natural state. I liken this process to scrubbing the hard drive of our computers to improve performance after one too many viruses diminishes its functionality. U.G. essentially felt that he had spent a lifetime seeking enlightenment and that in the end it was a waste of time, hence, the need to unlearn everything and start over. I have distilled a brief biography from several sources as, without knowing him, one is left to triangulate from varied opinions to develop a sense of his true character. If nothing else, U.G. certainly polarized the many individuals who crossed his path during his lifetime. I found Mahesh Bhatt's blog the most helpful, for he fills in the gaps of U.G.'s life that allow the reader to have an understanding of why he followed the path he did.[43]

U.G. was born on July 9, 1918, to Brahmin parents in Masulipatam, a town in coastal Andhra Pradesh, India, and raised in the nearby town of Gudivada. His mother died seven days after he was born and his father played no role in his life except the "hereditary role," as U.G. put it. Although they lived in the same town, they never lived under the same roof for any length of time. His father remarried soon after his wife's death and left his son to be cared for by his grandparents. Tummalapalli Gopala Krishnamurti was a wealthy Brahmin lawyer who gave up his practice to focus on overseeing U.G.'s education because his family believed that he had approached enlightenment in a past life. To that end, he was given a rigorous education in classical Hindu literature and was raised to become a great spiritual teacher; in a manner similar to J. Krishnamurti (we'll cover him later in this chapter).

Every day, from dawn to dusk, U.G. was made to listen to the Upanishads, Panchadasi, Naishkarmya Siddhi, the commentaries, and the commentaries on the commentaries. By the time U.G. reached his seventh year, he could repeat from memory most of the passages from these holy books. With this solid foundation in hand, he began to have life experiences that were opposite what the great holy books had taught him. First off, he began to doubt God as he felt his desire held sway over outcomes more than prayer. Another event he witnessed during these formative years was the brutal thrashing his grandfather gave to his great granddaughter after she interrupted a meditative session of the Esoteric Group of the Theosophical Society. "There must be something funny about the whole business of meditation," said U.G. to himself as he helplessly witnessed his grandfather savaging his own great granddaughter. "Their lives are shallow and empty. They talk marvelously. But there is a neurotic fear in their lives. Whatever they preach does not seem to operate in their lives. Why?"

In the year 1873, Helena Petrova Blavatsky, a Russian immigrant to the United States, along with Colonel Alcott, an American lawyer, founded the Theosophical Society. It was built largely on their reading of Buddhism and Hinduism and on a fusion of assorted occult presuppositions, what we would describe today as "New Age." For example, Blavatsky felt her clairvoyance could help her delve into the riddles of creation to discover the dormant power in man. It was open equally to believers and non-believers, as well as to the orthodox and the unorthodox. Being wealthy did not hurt your chances of moving up the hierarchical ranks of the organization. Ironically, the very reasons these folks railed against in traditional theological and secular circles found a happy home in this institution. We will delve more into some examples when we review the life of J.Krishnamurti later in this chapter.

At any rate, in those days, theosophy had a strong appeal to those who found little solace in orthodoxy and yet were not content to call themselves atheists. It attracted an articulate group of free thinkers and avowed atheists searching for some order and spiritual support. The Esoteric Society (or E.S. as it came to be called) was strictly for those who had proved their dedication to Theosophy. They were a secret group within the Society, and membership was offered to only those deemed to having the appropriate pedigree and having attainted the highest levels of self control and spiritual mastery. So you can imagine the impact on U.G. when he observed his grandfather behaving the way he did.

In the year 1932, when U.G. was fourteen, another event took place that steered him further away from the world of orthodoxy and tradition. Every year, he was made to fast on the anniversary of his mother's death. He was permitted to eat only at the end of the day after feeding a couple of Brahmin priests and washing their feet. He was also made to meditate and recreate in his mind, the image of his dead mother whom he had hardly seen. He was enraged that day when he discovered the Brahmin priests eating heartily in a nearby restaurant. "They too are supposed to be fasting. Enough is enough. They are all fakes," he said to himself. Furious, he raced back to his grandfather and, in an act of defiance, broke his sacred thread, the symbol of his religious heritage, and threw it away.

Between the ages of fourteen and twenty-one, he undertook all kinds of spiritual exercises. He practiced all the austerities. He was determined to find out if there was any such thing as *moksha*, about which all the great teachers of humanity had spoken endlessly. He wanted that moksha for himself. He had also resolved to prove to himself and to everybody that there cannot be hypocrisy in the people who have "realized" themselves. He searched for a person who was an embodiment of this realization.

He found a Hindu evangelist named Sivananda Saraswati. A strict and self-righteous "spiritual authority", U.G. spent seven summers in the Himalayas studying classical Yoga. While practicing Yoga and meditation, U.G. had every kind of experience talked about in the sacred books—samadhi, super samadhi, and nirvikalpa samadhi. "Thought can create any experience you want—bliss, beatitude, ecstasy, melting away into nothingness—all those experiences. But this can't be the thing, because I have remained the same person, mechanically doing these things. This is not leading me anywhere," thought U.G. to himself. His Yoga Master, Sivananda, was startled when U.G. caught him devouring some hot pickles behind closed doors. "How can this man deceive himself and others, pretending to be one thing, while doing another? He has denied himself everything in the hope of getting something, but he cannot control himself. He is a hypocrite. This kind of life is not for me." So he gave up his Yoga practice and left Sivananda.

As he moved into his adulthood, he became a cynic, rejecting the spiritual bonds of his culture and questioning everything for himself. He displayed a healthy contempt for his religious inheritance, a contempt that was to develop into an acute repugnance toward what he was later to call, "the hypocrisy of the holy business." By twenty-one, U.G. had become a quasi-atheist. He joined the University of Madras and for some years studied psychology, philosophy (Eastern and Western), mysticism, and modern sciences, but never obtaining a degree.

"There is a man at Tiruvannamalai called Ramana Maharshi. Come, let us go and see him. It is said that he is a human embodiment of the Hindu tradition," noted a friend to U.G. one day during the course of a discussion. By then, he had arrived at a point where he felt certain that all the teachers of mankind—Buddha, Jesus, Sri Ramakrishna, and so forth - had deluded themselves and deluded others. The description of that state, which these teachers talked about, had absolutely no relation to the way he was functioning. He had a revulsion, an "existentialist nausea," against everything sacred, everything holy.

In the year 1939, reluctantly, hesitantly, and unwillingly he went along with his friend to meet the famous sage of Arunachala. Bhagawan Sri Ramana Maharshi was reading comic strips when U.G. first saw him. At the very first glimpse of him, he thought, "How can this man help me?" As he sat there for two hours, watching the Bhagawan cut vegetables and play with this, that, or the other, he wasn't at all surprised to find that all those fancy assertions to the effect that this man's look changed you and that all questions disappeared in his presence, remained fables. "Is there," asked U.G., "anything like enlightenment?"

"Yes, there is," replied Ramana.

"Are there any levels to it?"

The Master replied, "No, no levels are possible. It is all one thing; either you are there, or you are not there at all."

Finally U.G. asked, "This thing called enlightenment, can you give it to me?" Sri Ramana did not answer. After a pause

U.G. repeated the question, "I am asking you whether you can give me whatever you have?"

Looking U.G. in the eyes, Bhagawan replied, "I can give it to you, but can you take it?"

"What arrogance!" U.G. thought to himself, "I can give it to you but can you take it?" Nobody had said anything like that before. Everybody that he had met before had advised him to do something. For seven years, he had been through all kinds of sadhanas. He had also gone through a "masochistic" period of self-denial. "If there is any individual who can take it, it is me. But what is that state? What is it that he has?" queried U.G. "He can't be very different from me. He was also born to parents. People say something happened to him. How do I know if there is anything like enlightenment? I must find out. Nobody can give me that state. I am on my own." U.G. never visited Sri Ramana again.

In 1941, he began working for the Theosophical Society. Shortly after, he began an international lecture tour on behalf of the Society, visiting Norway, Belgium, Germany, and the United States. Returning to India, he married a Brahmin woman named Kusuma Kumari in 1943, at age 25, and eventually fathered four children.

From 1947 to 1953, Krishnamurti regularly attended talks given by Jiddu Krishnamurti (again, no relation) in Madras, India, eventually beginning a direct dialogue with him in 1953. U.G. described one of their meetings as follows: "We really didn't get along well. Whenever we met, we locked horns over some issue or other. For instance, I never shared his concern for the world, or his belief that his teaching would profoundly affect the thoughts and actions of mankind for the next five hundred years – a fantasy of the Theosophist occultists. In one of our meetings I told Krishnamurti, "I am not called upon to save the world." He asked, "The house is on fire – what will you do?" "Pour more gasoline on it and maybe something will rise from the ashes", I remarked. Krishnamurti said, "You are absolutely impossible." Then I said, "You are still a Theosophist. You have never freed yourself from the World Teacher role. There is a story in the Avadhuta Gita which talks of the avadhut who stopped at a wayside inn and was asked by the innkeeper, "What is your teaching?" He replied, "There is no teacher, no teaching and no one taught." And then he walked away. "You too repeat these phrases and yet you are so concerned with preserving your teaching for posterity in its pristine purity." U. G. related that the two had almost daily discussions for a while, which he asserted were not providing satisfactory answers to his questions. Finally, their meetings came to a halt. He described part of the final discussion:

And then, towards the end, I insisted, "Come on, is there anything behind the abstractions you are throwing at me?" And that chappie said, "You have no way of knowing it for yourself." Finish – that was the end of our relationship, you see – "If I have no way of knowing it, you have no way of communicating it. What the hell are we doing? I've wasted seven years. Goodbye, I don't want to see you again." Then I walked out.

In 1955, U.G. Krishnamurti and his family went to the United States to seek medical treatment for his eldest son and stayed there for five years. In 1961, Krishnamurti put an end to his relationship with his wife. Their marriage had been a largely unhappy affair, and by that time, he described himself as being "detached" from his family, emotionally as well as physically. He left for London and then spent three months living in Paris, using funds he had obtained by selling his unused return ticket to India, during which time he ate a different variety of cheese each day. Down to his last 150 francs, he went to Geneva.

After two weeks in Geneva, he was unable to pay his hotel bill and sought refuge at the Indian Consulate. He was listless, without hope, and described himself as "finished." He requested that he be sent back to India, which the consular authorities refused to do at the state's expense. A consulate employee in her 60s named Valentine de Kerven offered him shelter. Valentine and Krishnamurti became good friends, and she provided him with a home in Switzerland.

For the next few years, the questions regarding the subject of enlightenment – or anything else – did not interest him, and he did nothing to further his enquiry. By 1967, however, he was again concerned with the subject of enlightenment, wanting to know what that state was, which sages, such as Siddhārtha Gautama, purportedly attained. Hearing that Jiddu Krishnamurti was giving a talk in Saanen, he decided to attend. During the talk, Jiddu described his own state, and U.G. thought that it referred to himself. He explained it as follows:

"When I listened to him, something funny happened to me – a peculiar kind of feeling that he was describing my state and not his state. Why did I want to know his state? He was describing something, some movements, some awareness, some silence.

In that silence there is no mind; there is action, all kinds of things. So, I am in that state. What the hell have I been doing these 30 or 40 years, listening to all these people and struggling, wanting to understand his state or the state of somebody else, Buddha or Jesus? I am in that state. Now I am in that state. So, then I walked out of the tent and never looked back.

Then – very strange – that question: What is that state? transformed itself into another question: "How do I know that I am in that state, the state of Buddha, the state I very much wanted and demanded from everybody? I am in that state, but how do I know?" The next day Krishnamurti was again pondering the question "How do I know I am in that state?" with no answer forthcoming. He later recounted that on suddenly realizing the question had no answer, there was an unexpected physical, as well as psychological, reaction. It seemed to him like "a sudden explosion inside, blasting, as it were, every cell, every nerve, and every gland in my body." Afterwards, he started experiencing what he called "the calamity," a series of bizarre physiological transformations that took place over the course of a week, affecting each one of his senses and finally resulting in a deathlike experience. He described it this way:

According to Krishnamurti, his life-story can be separated into the pre- and post-calamity parts. Describing his post-calamity life, he claimed to be functioning permanently in what he called "the natural state": A state of spontaneous, purely physical, sensory existence, characterized by discontinuity though not absence of thought. He also maintained that upon finding himself in the "natural state," he had lost all acquired knowledge and memories, and had to re-learn everything, as if "...the slate had been wiped clean."[44]

In spite of attaining this natural state at the age of 49, it seems to have left Krishnamurti rather forlorn and still quite cynical in the later part of his life until his death in March 2007. His life reminds me of St. Augustine, brilliant in its remarkable insights to our human existence but one that left him emotionally adrift, having reached the far shore feeling empty rather than fulfilled. I certainly do not detect a peaceful countenance in his Swan song, dictated in February of that same year. See what you think in these excerpts taken from those recordings.

What I have found of and by myself run counter to everything anyone has said in any field of human thought. They have misled themselves and misguided everybody. You still fall for all that because if, for instance, you were to change your diet you would die of starvation. But I want to live forever! Can you keep me alive and healthy, the way I have lived for ninety years of my life? No? But that's all that interests me! When once it throws out everything that has been put in there by your filthy culture, this body will function in an extraordinarily intelligent way. It can take care of everything.

If at any time I accept anything, it is not what the religious people have told me about the way the body functions, but what the medical doctors have found. Yet, what they do not know is immense; and they will never know how this body functions.

I have never taken any medicine nor have I ever seen a doctor. All the doctors who have advised me not to live the kind of life I had been living are now dead and gone. There is one exception. Once, I had typhoid fever when I lived in

Madras. My wife's brother was a top doctor in the General Hospital in Madras. The British had a wing in the hospital for themselves and nobody else was allowed to stay in the rooms in that wing. That year, however, they opened the wing to the general public. So my brother-in-law got me one room in it and another for my family members. In that room my wife and grandmother stayed. Three nurses took care of me taking turns every eight hours for a whole month, after which I walked out. Although I assert that all doctors should be shot, I don't advise others not to see a doctor. I don't know what I will do if I am in a situation where I want to prolong my life a little longer. So I would never tell others not to see a doctor. (Note: He did bring his son to America for polio treatment)

I brushed aside everything born out of human thought. Everything they told me falsified me. And what you are trying to get you can never get, because there is nothing to get. What you are is a belief; if you let one belief go, you must replace it with another; otherwise, you will drop dead. I am telling you, a clinical death will occur. It is not the near death experience of those 'near death' scoundrels. All those filthy religious people are fooling themselves and fooling everybody, living on the gullibility and credulity of people, making an easy living, selling shoddy pieces of goods and promising you some goodies that they can never deliver. But you want to believe all that nonsense. It's a reflection on your intelligence that you fall for all that crap to which you are exposed.

Nobody has given me the mandate to save you people or save the world. The human species should be wiped out for what it has done to every other species on this planet! It has no place on this planet. If I am sure of one thing, it is that. If it were not for your destructive weapons, you would have been wiped out a long time ago. And you are going to be wiped out, because now others have the means to wipe you out. But you are not going to go gracefully without taking every form of life on this planet with you. The human kind appeared on this planet and it thinks all this has been created for its use. You think you were created for a grander and nobler purpose. The human being is a more despicable thing than all the other forms of life on this planet. The native intelligence of the human body is amazing. That is all it needs to survive in any dangerous situation in life. The native intelligence is what you are born with; the intellect is acquired from what they teach you. So, you don't have any words or phrases, or even experiences, which you can call your own. You have to use that knowledge that has been put in there in order to experience anything.

There is nothing to your love: if you don't get what you want, what happens to your, "I love you darling, dearie, honey bunch, shnookie putsie, sugar britches, petite shu-shu, sugar booger?" If you don't get what you want out of all that, what happens to your lovey-dovey? The only test for me is money. How free you are with your money? I don't mean, "How wasteful you are with your money?"I have nothing to lose if the whole thing is wiped out. I have nothing to gain if it remains the same. The only relationship you have with anybody in this world is "What do I get out of it?" That's all you care about. Other than that, there is nothing to it! You all fool yourselves thinking that you are going to get something by hanging around me… ho ho ho! You're not going to get a thing because there is no need to get anything from anybody.

You can't fit me into any religious frame. I don't need to fool people and thrive on their gullibility and credulity. Why should I? I'm telling you, you will lose everything! You are not going to get anything from anybody. There is no need for me to say you're not going to get what you want from anyone else either. That you will find out by yourself. But that you can't do either by your own effort or by your volition or by anything you do or do not do. That is not something that happens in the field of cause and effect.

Everything was thrown out of my system. I don't know how I was thrown off the merry go round. I went round and round and round. I was lucky -- luck, not in the sense that when you go to a gambling place and win if you're lucky. They put me on a merry go round. I went on and on and on. I didn't have the guts to jump off. I was just thrown off like an animal thrown from the top of a tree. The animal just gets up and runs off.

Fear makes your body stiff, and then you will certainly break your limbs. My body is never stiff.

The demand for permanence -- permanent relationships, permanent happiness, and permanent bliss -- in any field and in any area of human existence is the cause of human misery. There is nothing to permanence. So don't be a damned fool! Go and make money. That's the only thing that impresses me – cash on the barrel! I told my grandparents this even as a little boy. I am in perfect harmony with this world exactly the way it is. I will never break the laws, no matter how ridiculous the laws are.

I am not a sociable man, yet I am not anti-social.

What I am trying to emphasize over and over again is that what has happened to me has nothing to do with the spiritual nonsense they preach; it doesn't have even a teeny weenie bit of spiritual content. It is a physical phenomenon pure and simple. Once this body is freed from the stranglehold of whatever is put in there either by spiritual teachers or secular teachers or by those scientists and medical technology, it functions in a very efficient way.

At the time I was born, when my mother introduced herself to me as, "I am your mommy," and hugged me and kissed me, I apparently kicked her, and she died in seven days after I was born. When they put me into the frame of an enlightened man, they said that the mother of such a child can never have any more children or sex, and that she would die. Actually she died of puerperal fever, but not because she gave birth to an enlightened man. They have to put such people into that frame of giving birth to an enlightened man.

There is no meaning in and no purpose to suffering. If a body is lucky enough to stumble into its natural way of functioning, it happens not through your effort, not through your volition; it just happens, but not by what you do or do not do. It is not even a happening within the field of cause and effect. "Acausal" is the most appropriate word for it, because a happening can never be outside the field of cause and effect.

If it stumbles into this of and by itself, such a body will be so unique that it will be unparalleled in this world and will function in an extraordinary way. Such a body has never existed before on this planet.

You don't have to take my word for it. Be miserable and die in your misery.

And such a man will be more spiritual than all the other claimants, but not in the ordinary sense of "spiritual," that nonsense must never be used. Spirit is only the breath as in "he breathed his last" the word has nothing to do with the spiritual crap.[45]

It is my humble opinion, that like Merton, his towering intellect and ego consumed him, and when someone becomes so self-absorbed, they disappear as in a black hole where nothing escapes, not even the light that was so obviously shining in his life particularly after his forty ninth year, if only he could have seen it. It's one thing to talk humility and another to walk it. Ego tripped.

The first thing, well two that is, one notices when visiting jkrisnamurti.org is the byline, "the official repository of the authentic teachings of J.Krisnamurti," and a pop up window soliciting donations. From what little I know of U.G. and J.K., the two that carried the mantle of Theosophy across the globe, I would think they would find this state of affairs amusing, repulsive, or perhaps both. Even with a basic understanding of their lifelong learning and wisdom was the fact that neither one felt a global organization should be left in their wake. U.G. was very clear on this point as noted above and in many of his writings and talks. He even held J.K. accountable for his sometimes blind faith in Theosophy in complete disregard of the tenets to which he espoused. He later broke his ties to Theosophy but not to his teachings. Although he indicated he was not important, speaking only as a conduit, he clearly felt he had something to say as evidenced in the legacy of the many support organizations and schools that exist today. J.K. is a conundrum wrapped in an enigma and it is doubtful anyone knew him well. The most glaring inconsistency can be found in one of his core teachings that "truth is a pathless land." The following excerpt provides J.K.'s reasoning for making this statement and can be found in its entirety on the Jkrishnamurti.org website.

The Order of the Star in the East was founded in 1911 to proclaim the coming of the World Teacher. Krishnamurti was made Head of the Order. On August 3, 1929, the opening day of the annual Star Camp at Ommen, Holland, Krishnamurti dissolved the Order before 3,000 members. The following is the full text of the talk he gave on that occasion: "We are going to discuss this morning the dissolution of the Order of the Star. Many people will be delighted, and others will be rather sad. It is a question neither for rejoicing nor for sadness, because it is inevitable, as I am going to explain. You may remember the story of how the devil and a friend of his were walking down the street, when they saw ahead of them a man stoop down and pick up something from the ground, look at it, and put it away in his pocket. The friend said to the devil, "What did that man pick up?"

"He picked up a piece of Truth," said the devil.

"That is a very bad business for you, then," said his friend.

"Oh, not at all," the devil replied, "I am going to let him organize it."

I maintain that Truth is a pathless land, and you cannot approach it by any path whatsoever, by any religion, by any sect. That is my point of view, and I adhere to that absolutely and unconditionally. Truth, being limitless, unconditioned, unapproachable by any path whatsoever, cannot be organized; nor should any organization be formed to lead or to coerce people along any particular path. If you first understand that, then you will see how impossible it is to organize a belief. A belief is purely an individual matter, and you cannot and must not organize it. If you do, it becomes dead, crystallized; it becomes a creed, a sect, a religion, to be imposed on others. This is what everyone throughout the world is attempting to do. Truth is narrowed down and made a plaything for those who are weak, for those who are only momentarily discontented. Truth cannot be brought down; rather the individual must make the effort to ascend to it. You cannot bring the mountain-top to the valley. If you would attain to the mountain-top you must pass through the valley, climb the steeps, unafraid of the dangerous precipices. So that is the first reason, from my point of view, why the Order of the Star should be dissolved.

In spite of this, you will probably form other Orders; you will continue to belong to other organizations searching for Truth. I do not want to belong to any organization of a spiritual kind, please understand this. I would make use of an organization which would take me to London, for example; this is quite a different kind of organization, merely mechanical, like the post or the telegraph. I would use a motor car or a steamship to travel; these are only physical mechanisms which have nothing whatever to do with spirituality. Again, I maintain that no organization can lead man to spirituality. If an organization be created for this purpose, it becomes a crutch, a weakness, a bondage, and must cripple the individual, and prevent him from growing, from establishing his uniqueness, which lies in the discovery for himself of that absolute, unconditioned Truth. So that is another reason why I have decided, as I happen to be the Head of the Order, to dissolve it. No one has persuaded me to this decision. This is no magnificent deed, because I do not want followers, and I mean this. The moment you follow someone, you cease to follow Truth. I am not concerned whether you pay attention to what I say or not. I want to do a certain thing in the world and I am going to do it with unwavering concentration. I am concerning myself with only one essential thing: to set man free.[46]

There are four global foundations charged with the task of ensuring his teachings are disseminated exactly as he intended. I have no idea how they skirt the issue that technically they should not exist based on his teachings, but there is a nefarious element to this lack of transparency that would make Hollywood executives salivate: J.K. wished to maintain absolute control not for the betterment of society but to maintain his pristine image.

In 1991, *Lives in the Shadow with J. Krishnamurti* was published by Radha Rajagopal Sloss, the daughter of Rosalind and Rajagopal Desikacharya. A good synopsis of the book can be found in an interview that Radha gave to Helen Tworkov writing for *Tricycle* magazine.

J. Krishnamurti mistrusted all religions and denounced the Eastern convention of deifying living spiritual masters. But by the time he died in Ojai, California, in 1986 at the age of 91, he had helped-perhaps more than anyone in this century to introduce Eastern teachings on the nature of mind to the West. In Lives in the Shadow with J. Krishnamurti (London: Bloomsbury Press, 1991), the prime subjects diminished by this mythic figure are the author's parents, the American-born Rosalind and Rajagopal, Krishnamurti's compatriot and dedicated associate; but the most compelling character is the shadow side of Krishnamurti himself. Radha Rajagopal

Sloss's book raises disquieting questions, and remains a refreshing alternative to the many hagiographic portraits proffered by Krishnamurti's devotees.

With delicacy, detail, and at times a painstaking attention to fair play, Radha Sloss addresses the confusion that arises when spiritual insight is presented and/or perceived in contradiction with daily life. Radha Sloss's mother was Krishnamurti's clandestine lover for some twenty-five years; and the slow dissolution of that romance was followed by a series of bitter legal battles over money and property initiated by the Krishnamurti Foundation and directed against Radha Sloss's father, Rajagopal. After administering to Krishnamurti's needs for over forty years as well as overseeing the editing and publication of his work, Rajagopal was shunned by the inner circle and accused by Krishnamurti of mismanaging money. Krishnamurti's rejection of Rajagopal was taken at face value by his close supporters, but the author convincingly portrays her father as the victim of a personal vendetta fueled by passions of the heart.

While retaining much of her childhood affection for Krishnamurti, who was a more active parent than her biological father, the most poignant anguish pervades the author's defense of her father. Yet the major drama of Krishnamurti's life was played out long before Radha Rajagopal Sloss was born. At age eight, Krishnamurti, a frail and dreamy child, lice ridden and open-mouthed, was discovered on a beach in South India and proclaimed by leaders of the Theosophical Society to be the next World Teacher. With exacting expectations, the Theosophists initiated the "coming messiah" into the spirit worlds with which they claimed to have direct contact. In addition, they introduced him to the mannered informalities of international society.

But at the age of twenty-nine, Krishnamurti rebelled. Refusing the role of the chosen one, he claimed that truth could not be approached by way of a teacher and that enlightenment rendered all belief systems equally and inherently useless. Helping others find their way in a pathless land became Krishnamurti's avowed mission for the next seven decades. During that time, he communicated his message in riveting language and provoked inquiries into human nature and the mind that were so fresh and compelling that his enlightenment and authenticity were affirmed for hundreds of thousands of people around the world. His books are printed in over forty languages, and of the fifty titles available in English, over thirty-five have sold more than 100,000 copies each. Yet, in a scenario that has become all too familiar to American Buddhist communities, Radha Rajagopal Sloss leaves us struggling to come to terms with the lives of our spiritual guides, and struggling as well with our personal investment in both the creation and destruction of their mythic dimensions.[47]

After this succinct introduction, the interview follows a Q & A format. I am only reproducing the 1st;

Tricycle: Some people have said that your portrait of a twenty-five-year love affair between your mother and Krishnamurti including three aborted pregnancies cannot be substantiated, that you have no proof and that no one can corroborate your story.

Radha Rajagopal Sloss: I was an eyewitness. When I started this book, I had planned to publish letters from Krishna to my mother, which I have and which corroborate what I say. But as you may know, the copyright laws have been changed. Published letters now need the consent of the sender or of that person's literary estate. I was not able to obtain permission to publish the letters; even if I donate them to a library, they will be available for research but not for publication.[48]

Now, one could argue ad infinitum on the veracity of her book, as indeed many have. I will simply say that J.K. never had the courage to admit to this affair, but ultimately the foundation did acknowledge it. Secondly, the fact that so much control is exerted over what is considered a legacy to humanity does cause one to pause and reflect. As Radha indicated, the affair was not as important as the lying and character assassination of her father. In line with J.K.'s teachings, it is up to us to ferret out the truth and any judgments we make on his contributions to insightful living.

I sense that J.K. struggled mightily with who he was. Groomed to be a sage, in essence, he became one, and that position led to his rejection of the hypocrisy that encrusted his life. Sadly, he never could break the ties from those that created him. The thought that so many idolized his every word and action created an environment where it is not possible to separate "teachings" from the "teacher." Ironically, the only thing that might have saved him was to go back to being a wandering savant on the beach where he was found. That step would take a massive dose of humility that seemed to be in short supply in the lofty circles of his acquaintances. Another ego tripped.

---

[43] Mahesh Bhatt (http://ug-k.blogspot.com/2007); http://www.sentientpublications.com/authors/ug.php; http://www.inner-quest.org/UG_R.htm; http://en.wikipedia.org/wiki/U._G._Krishnamurti

[44] U.G.Krishnamurti, The Natural State, First and Last Lecture given in 1972 at the Indian Institute of World Culture, Bangalore.

[45] My Swan Song, dictated by U.G. Krishnamurti to Louis Brawley, 2007, Vallecrosia Italy

[46] Jkrishnamurti.org

[47] http://www.tricycle.com/the-shadow-side-krishnamurti

[48] http://www.tricycle.com/the-shadow-side-krishnamurti

CHAPTER 18

SAFE HARBOR

Herman Melville pondered our fate in asking "where lies the final harbor from whence we unmoor no more?" I came across this passage after reading a short interview with Christopher Sheldon. *Where Lie's The Final Harbor* is the title of a book he was working on in 1996 about the life, a love story if you will, he shared with his wife.[49] I don't believe it was ever published, and Sheldon died in 2002 at the age of 76. That quote described his philosophy of life. "When you are on the sea of life, you never know where you are going to end up, how you are going to end up, and when you will end up. I believe you should give it your best and get as much out of it as you can." Sheldon was skipper of the 92-foot brigantine *Albatross* when the vessel sank suddenly on May 2, 1961, in a fleeting yet violent storm after leaving the Yucatan.[50] It was a teaching ship so most of the crew was in their late teens. Six of the eighteen people on board perished, including his wife.

As a metaphor for life, I can find no parallel to that of sailing. This insight is rather telling in that I was not born on or near the ocean and have only sailed a few times. One would not get far if I were at the helm. I suppose therein lies the lure. You have to know what you are doing when you grab the reins of a ship for the ocean can be quite unforgiving even for seasoned pros like Sheldon. In other words, you are held accountable for your actions; unlike most of life that allows us considerable wriggle room for deferring ownership to someone else. As we all too often note, the buck doesn't stop with the chief executive, who has a myriad of nefarious ways to abdicate responsibility while keeping all the spoils, or with spiritual sages, who rarely are held accountable for failing to live up to what they espouse. Life is unpredictable. It asks of us things that we do not want to pursue, nor wish to hear.

White Squall is the movie that chronicles the fateful events surrounding the *Albatross*. Although the movie was based on a true story, the lives of the characters who survived tell us as much about sailing the high seas of life as was portrayed in the film, which often strayed from the truth under the directorship of Ridley Scott. One telling story is that of Tod Johnstone, a survivor who actually played his father in the movie when it came out in 1996. According to Johnstone, his father offered little comfort when he returned home from that harrowing voyage, a frightened, shaken, seventeen year-old. "I had bumped around every boarding school in New England before sailing on the Albatross," said Johnstone. "I didn't get the parental attention I needed. It was sort of an escape from hell for me."

"My father saw the vessel's sinking as somehow related to his son's other shortcomings," said Johnstone, who was at the helm when the *Albatross* sank. So in the movie, I gave myself all of the love and energy my father wasn't giving me." [51]

One of the more ludicrous statements I've ever heard is that of being "a self-made person." I rarely speak in absolutes, but I don't think I've ever met anyone that has been alone from before they were born until the present day. We are all influenced beyond measure in every facet of our lives, both in our positive and negative attributes. What I will say is that moral support, having a guardian angel or someone in your corner, provides a deep well from which we can draw strength to shape our character in the same way we nurture our will.

The Latin phrase *Veritas vos liberabit* is a variant of *Veritas liberabit vos* (the truth shall set you free), verse 8:32 of the Gospel of John.[52]

On the surface, this statement seems to be the harbor we all seek in our lives, for it is self evident that indeed if we do know the truth we are free. However, like Pilate, who asked in verse 18:38, "*Quid est veritas*?" ("What is truth?") We often find ourselves adrift in attempting to ascertain it. In addition, the longer we live, the more we have to come to terms with the fact that not much in this life is at it is portrayed or what we thought it was. Hence, Augustine and Tolstoy represented most of humanity when they likened their plight to Tantalus and Aeneus, for the only fact that we can be sure of is that absolute truth is virtually impossible to discern. As humans, we love absolutes, as spiritual sages figured out a long time ago. That sensibility exists today in that it is virtually certain that a guru who espouses that they have the sure fire cure for the cancer of life will find a ready audience. If, on the other hand, I hold the opinion that there are no absolutes and that one must tread carefully in unchartered waters, I risk alienation for no one wants to be adrift at sea.

Ideally, by now we would have developed a "truth algorithm" that would spit out the likelihood a particular statement is true, an idea well beyond the latest and greatest lie detector technology. Unfortunately, for most of us, the absolute clarity this would provide as we navigate to our far shores is not available. Sometimes, our choices can result in very dire and real consequences as it did for those that sank on that fateful day. For the rest of us,

> *It comes down to one thing*
> *You can't run from the wind*
> *You trim your sails*
> *You keep going.* [53]

[49] The Day the Albatross Went Down, NY Times, by Jacqueline weaver, Published March 10,1996

[50] http://en.wikipedia.org/wiki/Albatross_%281920_schooner%29

[51] The Day the Albatross Went Down, NY Times, by Jacqueline Weaver, Published March 10,1996

[52] http://en.wikipedia.org/wiki/Veritas_vos_liberabit

[53] White Squall, 1996

CHAPTER 19

HARMONY IS MY HOME

Throughout history, there are many examples of human endeavors where humility is expressed in the way we conduct our lives. They illuminate for us how a single person's inner experience provides compelling motivation for larger communities to embrace the calling to something other than the status quo. Initially, one of the fundamental tenets of the original Rule of St. Benedict was universally to accept all as Christ. This imperative implied that if I as a ragged bum knocked on the door of an Abbey, I would be accepted as the embodiment of Christ and have my needs tended to. I would ask you to not test this rule today, for you would find that it is no longer the case. But imagine the "teachable moment" it created when it was practiced if you were the monk who answered the door. That's one sure way to put your theological training to the litmus test of human experience. Many would argue that it is no longer very practical to treat this Rule literally, and I suspect that's why St. Benedict felt drawn to add it in the first place. He knew it served as another tool in that proverbial toolkit that could be used to bend our will where it normally doesn't want to go.

Occasionally I am asked when I felt I was being drawn in a new direction. Initially, what came to mind was the experience I had in the Michigan bookstore, which I related earlier. Now I prefer to answer, "It began when I began." Perhaps my earliest days had little influence on my outlook today, but the evidence suggests that first impressions leave lasting imprints.

We toss around the words peace, love, and harmony like confetti so that the depth of their meaning is often lost. Using them can ring hollow, as has often been the case for me. Being described as "authentic" is another term bandied about with great frequency although it is most likely appropriate on rare occasions.

There are exceptions to every rule, and I can use the word "harmony" and "authentic" in at least once aspect of my life. I can state with certainty that I grew up in a place called Harmony Township on land once farmed by the Harmony Society. Society members, among many motivations, hoped to leave behind religious intolerance in their native Germany. They set up shop in Western Pennsylvania in what must have looked like the ancient forests of their homeland.

For whatever reasons, their way of life left an indelible mark early on my own perceptions of right living in contrast to my observations of the way most folks provided for themselves when I was growing up. A decaying cupola in my neighbor's woods, used for picnicking by the Harmonites as they tended their fields, was one of the few remnants to hearken one back to a time that wasn't in all that distant past. Except for the core village that was becoming a tourist destination, the bucolic scenery reminiscent of that spot has been all but replaced by the gritty landscape of the Industrial

Revolution. J&L Steel, a sprawling thirteen mile long edifice lay directly across the Ohio River from what was once Old Economy Village. Ironically, this economic juggernaut was to benefit the community for a relatively short period of roughly thirty years when the titans of industry found cheaper labor in the Far East to eradicate the hard fought living wage that many were beginning to earn. That entire plant was dismantled and reassembled in China, and there is now not a trace that the plant existed. However, to this day, the coal that fired the massive Bessemer furnaces still meanders its way up from West Virginia on rail cars en route to Lake Erie to make its way to coal fired plants and utilities across the globe. Each train consists of approximately one hundred twenty cars with a capacity of 120 tons each. Overflowing with raw energy, these long behemoths represent a gift that keeps on giving 24/7/365 for over 100 years from the primeval forests of Mother Earth. But I digress as that history charts a different course.

I have often used the Harmonites way of life as a benchmark of how we might actually live out the beach scenario I presented earlier. Yes, it is true that this community ultimately dissolved, but its legacy leaves a far better blueprint for what we as humans might strive for than the myriad of social "survivor series" models that we are left with in its wake. E.Gordon Alderfer, who helped establish the Peace Corps, offered this tribute to the Harmonites.

"In this day of vastly complicated societal mechanics, tremendously powerful governments, and the whole huge web of clashing world economies, we have very nearly lost all concept of the meaning of community. Human relationships are no longer generated by the spontaneous impulse of mutual cooperation, but rather take a long circuitous route through a complex labyrinth of social organization. When a man is unemployed in the little town down river, an overwhelming confusion of Federal, State and local machinery is set in motion before the helping hand of his fellow man can reach him. The personality of the community and its purpose, and the natural and spontaneous expression of love no longer form the dominant elements of the fabric of our social structure.

Yet, in all the long span of history, no nation or people have risen to a rich maturity either by predatory or violent means, or without that instinctive interweaving of individual efforts for the common welfare of the group which we call mutual aid. The individual instinct of survival is admittedly a great force, but before a social cohesion can be achieved the greater force of love and the instinct of mutual aid must have full play. And without cohesion a people and the permanent cultural products of a people are as nothing."[54]

John S. Duss, a descendant of the one of the founders of the Society, offered this capsule summary;

"The Harmonists built an agricultural, industrial, and commercial empire of enormous income, with resources totaling millions, and for 100 years their communal life, their business activities and their great wealth held the attention of the American public, arousing the interest of all, the admiration of many, and the suspicion, envy and cupidity of others"[55]

The bank I used, Old Economy, was founded by the Harmonites. The city of Beaver Falls, home of Joe "Willie" Namath fame, was platted for development through the bank's realty investments. Ironically, these results were achieved through an adroit economic system that isn't in the curricula of any executive MBA program. Essentially, the community produced just about everything it needed to sustain its people. Word soon spread that the quality of the goods produced were of high caliber, thereby creating a ready market for anything community members didn't need. In other words, money was removed as an internal trade barrier, being unnecessary except to purchase raw materials unavailable within. On the other hand, money flowed like honey into the coffers of the Harmonists who initially did not intend to create such a windfall.

Critics will readily point out that the Society ultimately disbanded proving that this system was unworkable. I posit that almost anything of note ever achieved goes through myriad of rebirths before a measure of success can be sustained. Furthermore, exploitation via the various *isms* with which we continue to experiment leave much to be desired in their wake, don't you agree?

An understanding of the Harmonites downfall gives us valuable insights to our nature and is a remarkable story in itself. Father George Rapp, as he became affectionately known, was the charismatic man who organized this flock and convinced many that the Promised Land lie east of their birthright in Europe. He was a simple vine dresser and weaver but was apostolic in his nature and zeal. He was intensely mystical, a fervent believer, an inspirer of souls, and he filled the hearts of his people with the faith and loyalty to carry on their difficult undertaking. On February 15th, 1805, their dream became reality as the articles of agreement were signed, land was purchased, and their journey began in earnest. However, one seed of their demise was sewn even before they set out on their trek in that they felt, certainly, Father Rapp did, that the world was soon coming to an end; therefore, thinking for the long haul was unnecessary. Yet we hold out hope that we will be better off following the calling of a charismatic who demands we leave everything behind. Why else make the journey, as it would be much easier to end your life and not continue.

This outlook was to be devastating, for community beliefs included leading a celibate life because there was no need for children in a world that wouldn't exist. It also fueled the raw sense of power of their leader, for he twice indicated the end was near and they needed to move on. This process entailed abandoning the first successful community to establish New Harmony along a pristine section of the Wabash in Southern Indiana and then to abandon this second successful community on his whim and return to what would become known as Economy. It is often asked, "What's in a name?" For the Harmonites, this moniker represented a high-water mark for the community. The decision to embrace the sword of capitalism by changing their name ensured that they would die by it as well.

The hierarchy of the Harmonites was such that decision making power was held by a group of Elders. In theory, they were elevated to these posts for their leadership acumen and wisdom. What we would call "transparency" today did not exist. The community at large trusted this group to do the right thing, and for the most part, this situation was the case as evidenced by the first two successful settlements.

This success inflated the ego of Father Rapp to the point he was becoming somewhat of a demigod. The second coming prophecy hadn't materialized because they weren't dead yet, but at the same time, he sensed he could harness the incredible advantage he had with the group of hardworking followers in his stable. Their growing stature had given him prominence well beyond their enclave, so off they went under his leadership to establish a new beachhead along the Ohio River roughly twenty miles from where their adventure began many years before. This time the motivation was to be close to the main center of commerce up river in Pittsburgh. Father Rapp had big ideas in mind, far from the roots of their sojourn to find peace and serenity in the new world.

Once, while visiting the beautiful community of New Harmony, I asked how it was that Father Rapp could get so many simply to pull up stakes, leave their magnificent homestead behind, and move again. "They had no choice," was the answer, for surrounding this oasis was a complete wilderness. Their livelihoods were intimately tied to the community they had created.

I don't think in his wildest dreams did Father Rapp imagine the financial success they were to experience when the community reestablished themselves in Western Pennsylvania. Contrary to the standard form of government economics today whereby we spend far more than we take in, Father Rapp had a cash cow in his pocket with money flowing in and only a minuscule amount flowing out. Without oversight, he and a few close associates had absolute control over this fortune. As they say, the root of all evil is money, and so it was for this group. I want to say that I don't think it was ever their intent to defraud anyone, but they simply succumbed to the power they wielded in the heady game of high finance. They invested heavily, held interests in land, businesses, and fine art, and most notably became substantial bondholders in railroads.

As a professor of mine once noted, "Debt equals slavery;" therefore, it wasn't long before the titans of Economy were easily outwitted by their nefarious partners in the big city, namely bankers and lawyers.

Meanwhile, there was growing discontent among the flock even though they were almost entirely in the dark about how their leadership had squandered their legacy. Some, however, knew things were terribly amiss, and the more vocal ones began demanding and receiving cash settlements with the intent of moving on.

In a way, a second coming did arrive for the community in the form of its demise at the hands of a leadership becoming what they had longed to escape. In spite of its failings, this community represented a shining example of what is possible when we embrace the nobler side of our humanity. Like a magnificent bridge, their existence spans what has come before and leads us to what is yet to come.

There are numerous other communities that embraced this ideal and some continue to exist, with the loftier goals so well articulated by Gordon Alderfer in his praise of the Harmonites. The Amana Colonies thrived until 1935 with similar values as the Harmonites. The Amana Society still manages some 26,000 acres held in trust, and Amana Refrigeration, creators of the iconic radar-range oven, is now a subsidiary of Whirlpool.

The Bruderhof, the legacy of Eberhard Arnold, continues to thrive to this day with communities around the world. Since the time of Christ, small groups of earnest Christians have tried to live by the ethics of the Sermon on the Mount; living as disciples in community has been a sought-for ideal. While many Christians have viewed these ethics for a time to come, others have insisted we were meant to live them in the here and now. It was Eberhard's firm belief that God could only intervene in our lives through the actions of people.[56] Arnold's life is a testimony that in community the Spirit, which can be found in all traditions, can reveal to us the real causes of social injustice.[57]

Of course, there are tens of thousands of monasteries that we can look at which provide guidance and insight to this way of life. Something that critics will point out is that across these communities one finds a general uniformity of shared values within the group; therefore, they do not reflect the reality of life beyond their structured enclaves. Frankly, I agree. Many communities have evolved from these beginnings to embrace ordinary life as we know it and do address in some respect this uniformity issue. There are secular groups, co-ops, and businesses organized around values beyond a common religious ideology or ethnic identity yet sharing aspects of those ideals of mutual aid for the betterment of all.

Arcosanti is an urban laboratory focused on innovative design, community, and environmental accountability. Its goal is actively to pursue lean alternatives to urban sprawl based on Paolo Soleri's theory of compact city design, Arcology (architecture + ecology). Built by over 7,000 volunteers since the commencement of the project in 1970, Arcosanti provides various mixed-use buildings and public spaces where people live, work, visit, and participate in educational and cultural programs.

Thousands of examples exist even in the brutal world of commerce. Volunteer Express is but one instance of a 100% employee owned company in business since 1973.

Dare I say that perhaps former President Richard Nixon said it best when he approved that Continuing Resolution affecting Native Americans, stating among other things that cultural pluralism is the source of a country's strength? That applies to families and communities as well and serves as a platform for us to continue to evolve with these beneficial characteristics intact yet recognizing that every grain of sand in the world is unique.

---

[54] E.Gordon Alderfer, Preface, The Harmonists; A Personal History by John S. Duss, 1943
[55] The Harmonists, A Personal History by John S. Duss, 1943
[56] Against the Wind, Forward by Jim Wallis to the book written by Markus Baum, 1998
[57] Thich Nhat Hanh, author, Love in Action.

CHAPTER 20

7...8...9...Its Time

What can boxing possibly offer in the way of insights to the destiny of humanity? I opine that, metaphorically speaking, everything. I reflect often over the gift I was given when a friend explained what was really going on in the "ring." It has stood the test of time, under all conditions, and it is easy to grasp. Do you remember that earlier thought on simplicity?

My friend's comment many, many years ago was, "Boxing is ninety-nine percent mental and one percent physical." I was, of course, somewhat incredulous, for it appeared to me to be a somewhat brutal form of sports entertainment. In fact, in many regards, it is just like life.

As with many of us, I often feel like I am a cog in a wheel, having no impact on essentially anything. In fact, in sorting out the meaning of life, the Creator would not have it otherwise because the range of human spirit can run from unfathomable depravity to sublime servitude. The element of "free will" is an "x" factor that allows us to explore all facets of this spirit. The challenge then thrown down before us is to sort this state of affairs out and move our lives to one of being "in service" rather than "out of service" to everyone but ourselves. This situation presents a rather unique challenge that at times seems hopelessly unsolvable or, conversely, that one is hopelessly naïve to think the puzzle pieces that make up our humanity will ever change. But as with the individual and community examples already outlined, we have seen that we can and often do rise above the conditions that we find ourselves in.

Typically, what befalls us is what has always taken us down. There's greed, ego, and lust to name but a few. When we are able to sublimate those elements of our character is when we are at our finest. As you are already aware, they can creep back in on us at a moment's notice or in some instances never leave us.

The "will" is the one attribute of our being that allows some of us to transcend our situations and enlighten the rest of us as to how we might do the same. Using the analogy of the Black Mamba mentioned earlier, I asked myself to consider the aspects of our human condition that we would least like to emulate, for it would stimulate finding the most likely therapeutic answer.

From the earliest historical records, we know that some humans sorted out that it was far more effective to break the will of another rather than simply to kill the offending individual. Torture is the option of choice when we want to send a clear message to those who survive or hear of it to adapt or face the same fate. Breaking the will is many faceted, so we find examples where it is attempted even when its intent is considered to be for the common good. Burning at the stake for heretical views or water boarding are two examples. When the historical record, right up to the present day, depicts this weapon as the tour de force from every imaginable corner of the globe, you know you have locked onto one of the holy grails of enlightenment. For if the will is broken, love, peace, harmony, and forgiveness do not exist.

Nurturing our will is something that is open to all, and it does not require extensive knowledge of anything or anyone but yourself. As I've written, even then we can stumble along quite miraculously in spite of ourselves. It is the single, most common, telling attribute I have found among folks from all walks of life, including the ones mentioned in this book and many, many other individuals I've encountered over the years.

Palden Gyatso survived twenty five years of interrogation and torture at the hands of the Communist Chinese as they systematically attempted to obliterate the Tibetan culture. Gyatso's will was never broken, and the Tibetan culture, although decimated, will live on, not because of his robes, his knowledge of monastic rituals, or his status, but from his will not to be dominated by another for what he simply believed. He bent his will to sustain what many of us could not. Thich Nat Hanh, Joan of Arc, St.Thomas More, Socrates, Guru Arjan Dev, Jacques Gruet, and Zeynab Jalalian are but a few of the millions who have shown that what we carry in our minds is more powerful than any weapon of mass destruction ever devised. A historical record exists for this luminous list. It does not include those that succumb to the subtle yet powerful psychological warfare carried out on the factory floor, the office, and our campuses daily.

As my friend intimated, no matter what happens, no one can take what's in your mind. I step into the "ring of life" as we all do. When I get knocked down, I have a choice each and every time to get back up for another round or stay down and capitulate to the dominate will at hand. I keep getting up, becoming a weapon of mass transformation on Salvation Beach and allowing others, by my example, to do likewise. I humbly hope this state of affairs is so for all of us.

CHAPTER 21

FORESHORTENING

How can it be that what we look to for guidance should divide rather than unite us? From corporations, governments, and the likes, it is to be expected that their interests and ours may not be aligned but theological clashes have had cataclysmic impact and continue to do so around the world today. As in the natural world, duality of purpose rears its head again, in both what we have gained and lost from our theological roots.

The answer to the question posed in the first paragraph is not just to satisfy academic curiosity. As I have intimated earlier, doctrinally correct theology can and has real impact on our everyday lives and often not for the better. This has been my own experience and has contributed greatly to divisions within my own family rather than being a haven for conciliation. I often chuckle when I hear a newscaster offer what is considered profound insight on some aspect of the Catholic faith. I can assure you that it is virtually impossible, for no one in Rome can possibly sort out the complexity of this vast organization and the many facets it presents to the world.

Vatican II was the last attempt to do just this, and in many respects, it has failed, leaving the Catholic Church not only differing from other theologies but also having great divides within it. It is not my intent to present a critical diatribe on the Catholic Church, for there have been many thousands of others who have taken a stab at it over the centuries. I will only submit that all Popes, infallible or otherwise, should be required to have a simple Q&A following an ancient practice, whose origins I can't recall, before accepting the role as shepherd to the flock. As a subtle but telling side note, a seemingly disheveled character whose demeanor and countenance appears to have never changed over the ions and is a remarkable look alike to Gandalf the White conducts questioning of the prospective Pope. In fact, no one really knows who the interrogator is and when asked, he simply says GW will suffice. The ensuing dialogue proceeds as follows:

"The Sistine Chapel is a remarkable edifice. Within this magnificent structure are held all the answers to the questions we may ever ask of you. In fact, you do not have to look at the walls, walk down the aisle or even stand at the altar. Raise your eyes to the ceiling and it alone is sufficient to the task. The legacy of Pope Julius II, who commissioned the painting, offers the incumbent all one needs to know about our capacity as humans for hypocrisy on a grand scale. Remember that humility is the antidote to ego and so we should be sufficiently graced with this attribute do you not agree?" As an aside, bear in mind that Julius II employed both Michelangelo and Raphael and the paintings they created represent some of the finest works of art the world has ever known. In my humble opinion, I give the definite edge to

Michelangelo, as Raphael was preoccupied with worldly vanity as was his patron.

GW continued, "The completed ceiling opened for the first time on October 31st, 1512. One of the very first paintings the Pope and his entourage would have viewed was, as his biographer Condivi noted, the most awe inspiring of the many hundreds of paintings they were to behold. In the direct line of sight was a depiction of Jonah between The Crucifixion of Haman and The Brazen Serpent. Painted on a conclave surface, Jonah leans back with his legs apart, his torso twisted to the right, and his head tipped up and turned to his left-a scene of struggle more akin to the body language of the ignudi than that of his fellow prophets. What most impressed Condivi was how Michelangelo created a *trompe l'oeil* through an incredible feat of foreshortening. He depicted the prophet in the act of leaning backward even though the painted surface curves toward the viewer, so that "the torso which is foreshortened backward is in the part nearest the eye, and the legs which project forward are in the part which is farthest."[58]As another side note, Goethe once commented, "Without having seen the Sistine Chapel one can form no appreciable idea of what one man is capable of achieving."[59] Back to the questioning GW continues, "This should inform you, my prospective Pope, that the sublime capacity of the individual to bend one's will, like foreshortening, cannot be proscribed but must be lived for then it becomes belief. This is what you will ask of your flock at all times. Does your own faith transcend your reality as depicted in this fresco?"

Moving on, GW notes that the controversy over the Last Judgment provides enlightenment with respect to character formation. The nudes depicted in this scene were painted over as part of what became known as "The Fig Leaf Campaign" by one of your predecessors. When they were later restored, Pope John Paul II aptly noted that nudity itself was not the issue, but only reflected a state of mind in the eyes of the beholder. What do you see?

The questioning is expected to produce appropriate responses to the queries, but the questioner is really studying the face of the candidate for signs of anxiety and to peer at his eyes, for the eyes are a gateway to the heart, and when it is humbled, only the "truth" is revealed on the surface.

The institutional church, like the Black Mamba, as in all theological hierarchies, or governments and corporations for that matter, holds in its grasp a duality of nature whereby the organizational capacity to embrace humility is limited only by the individuals within it to practice what they preach. But to whatever greater or lesser degree they achieve this quality does not allow for me to abdicate what I do as an individual.

Of the many writings of Thich Nhat Hanh, "Going Home" is a comparative study of the similarities between Jesus and Buddha. There are myriads of other books, symposia, seminars, retreats, and councils that explore common ground but in the end, each group tenaciously holds to their respective turf. No one need look far to validate this claim, as religious turmoil is more likely a common denominator than conciliation. As I mentioned earlier, just one word can change the consciousness of a community, so I would offer that religious and government leaders refrain from using the word "tolerance" to define a sense of community among theological rivals. When I tolerate something in my life, I am acknowledging the fact that I may live with a situation that I really don't want to. It does not imply compatibility, humility, or compassion to another's point of view.

Essentially, theological perspectives cultivated over the millennia and the thoughts I shared earlier in this book have led me to conclude that once again, we as individual grains of sand have the capacity to be as transformative to these institutions as much as they ever might hope to be for us. It's easy enough to test ourselves, and why not, for an institution is made up of individuals, right? If you can't make it to Rome to see it firsthand, simply type in "depiction of Jonah on the Sistine Chapel ceiling" into any Internet browser. See if you can fool GW when it's your turn to be questioned.

---

[58] Michelangelo and the Popes Ceiling, Ross King , 2003, p297
[59] Johann Wolfgang Goethe, 23 August 1787

CHAPTER 22

REMISSION

I stumbled across the Latin root, *remissionem*, for the word forgiveness. I prefer this translation, for it is often associated with a positive outcome in relation to cancer treatment. It usually represents a transitional phase as in we're not really sure if it's gone or will return.

So it is with forgiveness in life. We read and hear much about love and forgiveness as being essential elements to our wellbeing, but taking an abstract concept and putting it into practice can leave us wanting, for the results often fall short of our expectations. We may know when we are "in love," but the signs are not always obvious when forgiveness exists in our hearts.

One individual whom I've come to admire is St. Francis of Assisi. Now St. Francis is legendary and venerated by millions for sometimes quite different reasons. Mine are twofold. First, he remained resolute in his beliefs throughout his life. What we today would describe as being "authentic." The second, one of those resolutions involved adherence to disavow ownership of anything, for he was keenly aware of how our wants and desires can corrupt us.

"Illuminato has asked Francesco if he may have a Psalter."

"You know it is against our rule," Francesco says, "for any friar to possess more than one tunic, quilted if he likes, a cord, and breeches?"

Illuminato replies, "Yes, Father."

After a moment's pause, Francesco continues, "If you own a Psalter, then you will want a breviary. And when you have a breviary, you will sit in your stall like a grand prelate and say to your brother, 'Hand me my breviary'."[60]

For those of you unfamiliar with Francesco's grand entre to his own salvation, here it is. During prayer at a dilapidated church at San Damiano, God spoke to him from a crucifix, bidding him to repair the church. Francesco took some bolts of cloth from his father's warehouse, sold them, and delivered the profit to the resident priest to pay for the repair of the chapel. Pietro, enraged by his son's extravagance, brought a complaint against him, which was resolved in the public square of Assisi. When the bishop advised he return the money to his father, he declared, my Lord Bishop, not only will I gladly give back the money that is my father's but also my clothes. He stripped off his clothes, placed the money on them, and standing naked before the bishop, his father, and all present, announced, "Listen, all of you, and mark my words. Hitherto I have called Pietro Bernardone my father, but because I am resolved to serve God, I return to him the money on account of which he was so perturbed and also the clothes I wore which are his, and from now on, I will say, 'Our Father who art in heaven,' and not Father Pietro Bernardone." [61]

To me, this declaration goes to the heart of the sometimes treacherous and conflicted path our journeys can lead us on. Ultimately, as I stated earlier, many of us admire what

St.Francis came to represent through his life, yet he broke two of the Ten Commandments of his faith to honor a third. Is it perhaps like a "just war," where the end justifies the means? More importantly, did he ever ask forgiveness (or forgive for that matter) his renounced real father and heartbroken mother? No one I have ever asked or anything that I have read thus far suggests that he did.

The last years of St. Francis' life were bittersweet, for the path of salvation that his life represented and that endeared so many early followers could not be sustained. In fact, the Order of Lesser Brothers he founded, then numbering in the thousands, had fractured into two groups: those who actually tried to emulate his life and those that couldn't but still wanted the benefits of aligning themselves with his personae. "Poverty Lite" might be an apt description for them. Within a few years of his death, Brother Leo, one of his close companions, wrote the *Mirror of Perfection* as a defense against those in the Order who were opting for something less than perfect. To wit;

The writer of this book has evidently undertaken to set forth what he considered to be the actual intention of St. Francis regarding the observance of poverty, in opposition to those whom he considered traitors to the Saint and his ideal. His book bears the impress of a soul highly indignant with the false brethren who were betraying the Lady Poverty. Evidently, at the time when the work was written, there was hot controversy in the Order between the Relaxed Brethren and the Spiritual or Observant Brethren, and the writer is one of these latter. Nevertheless, the book bears in parts the genuine regard of the earliest Franciscan spirit with its zeal for

poverty and with its simplicity. These chapters might be aptly
described as the story of St Francis' Passion, written by one
who entirely entered in spirit into the bitter disappointment
experienced by the Saint during the last three or four years of
his life when he saw so many of the friars following Brother
Elio and his compeers in the ways of ambition and
worldliness in disregard of the original simplicity of the
Franciscan vocation. It is sad reading and yet very
wholesome, for it reminds us how the flesh is ever rebellious
against the spirit and apt to mar the most spiritual movements
and how the worldly spirit is ever in conflict with the Spirit of
God wherever the Spirit of God is found. There are those who
are scandalized when they discover imperfection in a religious
body of men, but healthy minds see only the inevitable
conflict which must arise when a spiritual ideal comes into
close contact with the earth and they are edified even if
humbled.[62]

Brother Elio fascinates me, for he represents the
quintessential successful person of today in all of us. He has
become such a chameleon so that when he looks in the mirror
he becomes the personae of what in reality he is not. The
mirror no longer plays the reflective role to cast a shadow on
what he (or we) has become. He hobnobbed with the rich and
famous; soliciting vast sums of money, something he was
forbidden to touch, in order to build a magnificent church to
honor Brother Francesco upon his death. Begging for food
was not his style either, for he personally oversaw the
preparation of lavish meals. Of course, the powers to be felt
he had all the "right stuff" to appoint him the head of the
Order when St. Francis died.

Therefore, we have on the one hand Brother Francesco who was so well respected that even Sultan al-Kamil gave him safe passage, in the middle of a crusade no less, to dialogue over Islam vs. Christianity. At the same time, he was leading a fracturing organization that felt it imperative not to live like he did so it could survive into the next millennium as it has done handily I might add.

My thought is that we cannot attain "perfect" forgiveness just as no one could actually live like St. Francis. Don't forget, I'm not sure he was as perfect as we like to think. I mean if you preach love and forgiveness as your basic tenets, it seems as though a good starting point to practice on would be your own family. That can be the greatest challenge as many of us already know. Poverty of the spirit knows no bounds.

Recently, I heard the story of a playwright. He had his share of drama growing up with an abusive father and in contrast a caring mother. As an adult, inspired by drama of the stage, he scraped together over $10,000 to put on his first major play. It flopped, and he lost everything. In the ensuing years, still playing a role in his personal transformation, he had forgiven his father. He decided to put on the same play that failed years earlier; it turned out to receive great reviews and performances started to sell out. Of course, it wasn't exactly the same play, for that act of forgiveness played a healing role not only at home but also carried on to the stage. Years have passed and he is now in a reverse role and caring for his father. The interviewer asked him if his father had ever acknowledged his behavior. We are conditioned to expect this in our lives where all the unraveled loose ends are neatly tied off, but contrary to our expectations, he indicated that never occurred, for it simply wasn't in his father's makeup to offer or expect it.

To me, this dialogue exemplifies how forgiveness plays out in our everyday lives. As much as we would like to, we can't control the outcome of someone else's behavior by our actions, but failure to act on our part allows that cancer to grow, and we never have the opportunity for remission to hold sway over our hearts. Personally, I have never experienced a time when I've allowed anger or hate to hold sway as a pathway to soothing my soul. The very idea of "remission" is that it leaves open the possibility of my regression as quite frankly often occurs. My simple awareness of the fact that forgiveness is not an absolute but one of the many nuanced behaviors the Creator has endowed us with as we journey out of darkness. It requires constant vigilance to nurture. It is not easy, but once again, available to all regardless of creed or lack thereof.

What do you think?

---

[60] Scripta Leonis referenced in Salvation, Valerie Martin p97

[61] St Francis of Assisi Omnibus of Sources referenced in Salvation, Valerie Martin, p5

[62] The Mirror of Perfection attributed to Brother Leo, translation from the Latin by Constance De La Warr. Intro by Father Cuthbert, O.S.F.C.

CHAPTER 23

UP BY THE RIVERSIDE

Harry Emerson Fosdick, first pastor of historic Riverside Church located in NYC observed, "Prophetic, germinative ideas are here; there are open doors of possibility for good as well as evil." Pastor Fosdick must have developed this succinct insight from his own life experience. The Presbyterian Church hierarchy had decided to put him on trial for what were considered his modernist views that strayed too far from their fundamentalist origins. However, having friends in high places ensures positive outcomes from life's theological landmines, and none other than John D. Rockefeller, a Baptist, plucked Harry from the pit bulls when he made him pastor of the imposing edifice he was creating on the upper west side along the Hudson river. I am certain all the characters of a Shakespearian classic exist in this church whose primary role is to advocate for the poor and disenfranchised.

In an unusual living arrangement, I was for a time ensconced within a stone's throw of the gargoyles and other lofty projections that made up the façade of this structure. At that early stage of my life, I was not sufficiently knowledgeable with respect to the insight of Pastor Fosdick's quote, but was simply drawn to the more pragmatic, yet perhaps loftier, ideals chiming from the bells. The roof of the Union Theological Seminary, upon which I was able to walk out on from my apartment, would seemingly vibrate in sync with the thunderous projection of salvific sounds emanating from these towers.

Paul Tillich, famed Protestant theologian may have been holding classes under my feet as I trod across the roof. I know I walked across his grave, for his ashes are spread over a pine grove in New Harmony, Indiana. In fact, one Jane Owen, New Harmony resident until her passing in 2010, may have been in his class at that time. Her husband's ancestors had purchased New Harmony from the Harmony Society when they vacated it. He intended to set up a sectarian community patterned after the Harmonites, but it managed to thrive for only a few years. However, it was to remain a haven for an eclectic mix of folks seeking alternative Utopias in one form or another. Jane could well indulge her interests having hailed from a family that owned both Standard Oil (now ExxonMobil) and Texaco. I was able to meet her through an acquaintance after I had responded to an ad posted in a grocery store for a retreat that was held on the grounds. We held a mutual interest in the history of the Harmony Society.

Common ground, interests, and the strands of life woven in a fragmentary tapestry create a foundation of hope transcending all in its path. I am nearly awake to its call, for it beckons loudly now.

"No man is an Iland, intire of it selfe; every man is a peece of the Continent, a part of the maine; if a Clod bee washed away by the Sea, Europe is the lesse, as well as if a Promontorie were, as well as if a Mannor of thy friends or of thine owne were; any mans death diminishes me, because I am involved in Mankinde; And therefore never send to know for whom the bell tolls; It tolls for thee."

Devotions Upon Emergent Occassions, XVII, 1624, John Donne

TRUE OF ONE & ALL

Some time ago, I don't recall exactly when, I came to realize that my thoughts and life were not as unique as I had envisioned. Although influenced by a myriad of factors, much of what I have experienced is similar to many others. It's humbling at first, but ultimately, this insight helps to illuminate our greater calling as part of the whole of humanity. The more we find similarities among ourselves, the more likely it is that we find that elusive peace and prosperity in life.

It was the same with the process of writing this book. As I've already mentioned, I felt connected with what someone had already said, written, or experienced a hundred or perhaps thousands of years ago. At the same time, there are points of departure that form the basis for the next generation to struggle with on our everlasting journeys.

One of the most poignant examples would be that of the life Dr. R. M. Bucke who lived from 1837 to 1902. The quintessential "renaissance man," he had many interests, one of which cost him a foot and several toes as he hiked across the mountains of California after mining for silver. The death of his mother left him enough of an inheritance to pursue collegiate studies. Ultimately, his career in psychiatry led him to become the provincial for the Asylum for the Insane in London, Ontario, where he remained for most of his life. He is most noted for the book Cosmic Consciousness in which he espouses his own theories on the expanse of our human journey. The book covers his personal spiritual path, as well as that of many others that he came across in his practice.

He felt that there were three levels of consciousness encompassing all of life: simple, which covered both humans and animals; self, which was unique to humans; and cosmic, which was what some had already achieved but for most of humanity remained elusive. Early on, he felt that science held the answer to the mystery of our existence as the next evolutionary step evolving out of religious roots. He was to come full circle in this regard and, ultimately, came to believe that mystics with a vision of our role in the greater cosmos of the universe came closer to the mark.

He sensed that a common heritage lay beyond the great theological divides up to that point in history. He also felt that the airplane would become one of the great equalizes of his day, playing a prominent role in eradicating poverty. At one point, he seemed preoccupied with determining the age at which we might most likely have a glimpse of enlightenment, which he was trying to pinpoint at around thirty. He had to revise that theory when he came across C.M.C. Her story, along with several others, became part of the book but to protect her privacy he only used initials. What appeared was an account, captured in her own words, of her mystical experience. I highly recommend you read the complete version as paraphrasing her thoughts does not capture the essence of the agony and ecstasy of her journey. I am only reproducing a few passages here.

C.M.C. passages

I was born in the year 1844. I cannot remember a time when I did not think and wonder about God. The beauty and sublimity of nature have always, from early childhood, impressed me deeply.

How terribly I felt when I learned that without the gospel the heathen could not be saved. The cruelty and injustice of it made me almost hate God for making the world so. I joined the church, however, thinking that it might bring me peace and rest; but although feeling safer I was just as far as ever from being satisfied. The vastness and grandeur of the God which I felt in nature I could never reconcile with the God in the Bible, try as I would, and of course I felt myself a wicked skeptic in consequence.

So it went on and though to all appearance I was happy and full of life like other girls, there was always that undercurrent--a vein of sadness deep down, out of sight. My experience was no doubt ordinary--largely that of the average girl living the average commonplace life--with aspirations and ideals to all appearance beyond any hope of fulfillment. At twenty-two I was married. Ten years later a change of place broke up the scene. From that time, without my going very deeply into the subject, a general idea of evolution was gained, and immortality, etc., were left for scientific research to discover, if to be discovered at all. My attitude was that of an agnostic.

There I rested, not altogether content, it is true. Something in life had been missed which it seemed ought to be there; depths in my own nature which had never been sounded; heights I could see, which had not been reached.

Walt Whitman, in "Leaves of Grass," had portrayed with wonderful power and sublimity this phase of mental and spiritual development, as those who look deeply into their own natures must see. In those wonderful poems nature herself utters her voice, pouring out the elemental pain and passion in living, burning words as lava is poured in torrents from the crater of a volcano--not his voice alone, but that of the soul of humanity imprisoned, struggling to break the bonds which enclose and hold it in. How sweet to lean upon that great soul! To feel that tender human sympathy! And seeing what heights he had reached, and knowing the road he had traveled, what courage!

At last, subdued, with a curious, growing strength in my weakness, I let go of myself! In a short time, to my surprise, I began to feel a sense of physical comfort, of rest, as if some strain or tension was removed. Never before had I experienced such a feeling of perfect health. I wondered at it. And how bright and beautiful the day! I looked out at the sky, the hills and the river, amazed that I had never before realized how divinely beautiful the world was! The sense of lightness and expansion kept increasing, the wrinkles smoothed out of everything, there was nothing in the entire world that I let go! Carpenter tells us that the "suppression of thought" and the "effacement of projects and purposes" are the chief things insisted upon by the Indian experts or yogis in the attainment of the Siddhi or miraculous powers (meaning illumination-- Nirvana). The same doctrine has evidently been taught in

India for ages. In the Bhagavad Gita it is laid down that the "working of the mind and senses" must be restrained--that, in fact, an absolute mental vacancy or blank is the condition in which to receive illumination. This seems to be the basis of the teaching of Jesus, that we shall not allow ourselves to be preoccupied with care for money, food, clothing, and household need. But one thing is needful, he says: Nirvana, the kingdom of God. And worrying about these worldly matters only tends to keep us from that, while if we attain to the worldly things which we seek nothing is gained, for they are valueless. So Balzac says: The self conscious life "is the glory and scourge of the world; glorious, it creates societies; baneful, it exempts man from entering the path of specialism, which leads to the Infinite." And Whitman: "What do you seek"? "Do you think it is love?" "Yes," he continues, "love is great, but there is something else very great: it makes the whole coincide; it is magnificent, beyond materials, with continuous hands, sweeps and provides for all." If you have that you want nothing else. Oh, I thought, if this is what it means, if this is the outcome, then pain is sublime! Welcome centuries, eons, of suffering if it brings us to this! And still the splendor increased.

Deep in the soul, below pain, below all the distraction of life, is a silence vast and grand--an infinite ocean of calm, which nothing can disturb; Nature's own exceeding peace, which "passes understanding." That which we seek with passionate longing, here and there, upward and outward, we find at last within ourselves. The kingdom within! Indwelling God are words whose sublime meaning we never shall fathom.[63]

Bucke also made connections with the thoughts of Dante, Buddha, Mohammed, Christ, Yepes, Behman, and many others. In particular, he held a great affinity for Walt Whitman whom he befriended. At the same time, he found institutional theology quite limiting. He wrote, "All readers of this book will have noticed the apparent incompatibility between the so-called religions--in other words, the churches--and Cosmic Consciousness. The man who enters or is to enter the latter either never belonged to a church, as Walt Whitman, or leaves the church before illumination, as C. M. C. did, or immediately upon illumination. Almost the only exception to this rule was John Yepes--an exception to be explained by the great breadth of the Catholic Church, which allowed him to interpret his experience in terms of the current religion. Churches are inevitable and doubtless indispensable on the plane of self consciousness, but are probably (in any shape) impossible on the Cosmic Conscious plane."[64]

Burke's humility, the precursor to any worthwhile insights, comes through from the very beginning of the book in his dedication to a son lost to an accident in the previous year. Only a portion of the letter appears here.

DEAR MAURICE:

A year ago today, in the prime of youth, of health and of strength, in an instant, by a terrible and fatal accident, you were removed forever from this world in which your mother and I still live. How at the time we felt your loss--how we still feel it--I would not set down even if I could. I desire to speak here of my confident hope, not of my pain. I will say that through the experiences which underlie this volume I have been taught, that in spite of death and the grave, although you are beyond the range of our sight and hearing, notwithstanding that the universe of sense testifies to your absence, you are not dead and not really absent, but alive and well and not far from me this moment.

Only a little while now, and we shall be again together and with us those other noble and well-beloved souls gone before. I am sure I shall meet you and them; that you and I shall talk of a thousand things and of that unforgettable day and of all that followed it; and that we shall clearly see that all were parts of an infinite plan which was wholly wise and good. Do you see and approve as I write these words?

Because of the indissoluble links of birth and death wrought by nature and fate between us; because of my love and because of my grief; above all because of the infinite and inextinguishable confidence there is in my heart,

I inscribe to you this book, which, full as it is of imperfections which render it unworthy of your acceptance, has nevertheless sprung from the divine assurance born of the deepest insight of the noblest members of your race.

So long dear boy![65]

---

[63] Cosmic Consciousness, Richard Maurice Bucke, [1901]
[64] Cosmic Consciousness, Richard Maurice Bucke, [1901], p324
[65] Cosmic Consciousness, Richard Maurice Bucke, [1901] i,ii

NOTHING LEFT BUT RIGHT

I can't identify an exact moment when the urge to write appeared on my radar, but I do distinctly remember that I felt I would not commit to anything definite until my life was in order. My thinking was that I could hardly write of wisdom attained if my actual life did not reflect it. After quite some time had passed, I realized this line of reasoning was not leading to any obvious endpoint, for my thoughts remained in abeyance, for my life still seemed to be sailing to that ever receding shore that taunted Aeneus. How is one to know if one has arrived at that proverbial far shore? A great tragedy, monumental triumph, or perhaps stellar careers are but three compelling scenarios that may lead us to believe we have arrived and that peace will be ours.

In the writing of this book, I have used many compelling stories that others have told or lived as they have had a great impact on my life. I have only sparsely interspersed those "one liners" that fill many spiritually related texts. As I mentioned earlier, I seemed to have been suffering from anecdotal overload, and what was meant to inspire or provide succinct insight, in reality was dulling my senses. It could be simply that this is a reflection of poor memory or perhaps that I seemed to draw more from sketches that encompassed the continuum of a life experience.

"Life is what you're doing while you're planning your life" is one of those exceptions to this rule as I do catch myself repeating it to others or falling back on it for support since it was first told to me many, many years ago by an acquaintance of mine. I really don't recall the context of our discussion, but the words have stuck around to help shape the mosaic of who I am. And so it is with the writing of this book, in that while I was waiting for divine inspiration ala the Bodi tree of Buddha, I came to the realization that a pinnacle point of enlightenment was unlikely to occur. In reality, this may have been the most insightful thought that ever occurred to me. Unlike many sages that we revere for one reason or another, I am not one of them. I have no special gifts, am not descendent from aristocracy, and have no capabilities to woo the masses like the golden tongue of Chrysostom. Yet, like Achilles' soft spot, I do feel I have stumbled across a path that most of us can identify with in our daily lives in pursuit of our unique redemptive paths. Perhaps flying under the radar undetected is what gives us the vision to see what has eluded so many.

If I desire anything, it is the hope that I have conveyed that however far from shore you perceive you are, you may actually be closer to home than you think. When you dive under the hood of all the greatest spiritual sages who have ever existed, you find, flawed, sometimes severely, human beings. Behind the great institutions that owe their existence to spiritual masters of one swipe or another, we find intrigue, calamity, scholarship, and cruelty as they forge ahead to make their mark on our daily lives. Make no mistake, if they can and have continually remade their history to insure redemption and survival, surely they can offer no less for the flocks under which they hold sway.

In this context we begin to glimpse the Creator's grand plan and the infinitesimally small, yet vital, roles we play in its unfolding.

CHAPTER 25

A LOVE IN TIME

What might it take to peer beyond the blinding light of our temporal existence? Perhaps it's a genetically reengineered new life, ingots of gold in a Swiss bank vault, or the adulation and respect of millions. Or how about having all the wisdom of all the sages at a moment's recall, a photographic memory of all the sacred texts ever written, or maybe the gift of Michelangelo in your hands?

I suspect that if you knew anyone that might have any of the above attributes, and you asked them if they had found peace, they might answer, "Well, quite honestly, not really, for it never seems to last for very long."

One year, I received a present from my oldest daughter that had a profound impact on my being from the first moment I looked at it. It was in retrospect, the right key, to the right door, at the right time, an "aha" moment. It was a collage, in calendar form, of some of the events in our lives. These fragmentary moments that ultimately compose "a life" quite possibly give us the most compelling evidence of that elegant simplicity we hoped to find when we began our journey. Perhaps what we have sought, whether it has been through the lens of Tolstoy, Augustine, Buddha, or the myriad of many, many others, is an elevated plane of existence that does not exist. That is why so many of them, at the end of their lives, and we in the present, still feel an emptiness or loss for not having achieved perfection in our inner and outer experience of life as we have lived it. Fragments, however, whether of baseball highlights, beautiful arias, crucifixions, birthday parties, or holding the hands of a loved one, can over time grace us with endless moments that ultimately form a continuum that will indeed enlighten us. For it is through these moments that we are given the opportunity to peer into despair, hope, forgiveness, and love. Like gravity, we remain suspended in the balance of life as it evolves. At once, we can sense the beauty in all things, however tragic or joyful, and the meaning of life is held out before us.

If you have ever had the opportunity to be in Washington, DC as the cherry trees blossomed, what would be the response if you walked up to one of them and asked, " Why are you here, why are your blossoms so beautiful, and why do you fill the air with sublime sweetness?" To those, humbled in stature to be but a grain of sand, one might hear the "truth" revealed in the trees response, "And do you not exist as I, where what you offer is for the benefit of any that might cross your path? Some of us in this grove have been damaged or destroyed by storms while the rest of us carry on for as long as it is our calling to do so."

The natural world and our senses to experience it provide us as good an insight as any I've ever come across to answer the riddle of our existence. As we are part of the natural world, it would only make sense (no pun intended) that this would be the case. As humans, we do have complex emotions that can obscure these basic facts as the last few thousand years of recorded history has shown. We are also well endowed with the ability, over time, to reconcile ourselves first to ourselves and then to those around us.

I draw strength from my own "life moments" to carry on and adjust my path to reach that far shore, now knowing I am already there. Every instance of anger, mistrust, or fear that I now experience can be neutralized with the realization that I'm not here for very long. Historically speaking, no one will remember our stupidity on a given day when we succumbed to the status quo, but like the cherry blossoms, our legacy for acts of forgiveness and love will last forever.

William Blake wrote this poem that elegantly captures in a few lines the essence of the fragmentary nature of our existence and our senses;

Man has no body distinct from his soul;

For that call'd Body is a portion of Soul

Discover'd by the five senses, the chief

Inlets of Soul in this age.

Honoring R.M. Burke, I humbly offer to you the reader this book. Full as it is of imperfections that render it unworthy of your acceptance. I remain hopeful that in some way it offers solace and support wherever your redemptive path leads you. There is a case to be made by some that the great struggle of our time is that of "mass" humanity vs. the "singular" needs of one individual. To me they are the same as individuals determine the trajectory humanity will follow. I believe the fragmentary moments of our lives capture the essence of our higher self. Moreover, when we are graced with the humility to see this in all things at all times we then know that my love is your love, my dreams are your dreams, and my loss is your loss. And for all time, the Creator harkens us to stay the course as *My Hope Is Yours*.

ABOUT THE AUTHOR

Paul holds a degree in Electrical Engineering from the University of Pittsburgh. His multifaceted career and interests have allowed him to engage with folks from all walks of life. These rich experiences have provided the strands from which he began to see the fabric that binds us all regardless of our station. When he was but a young boy, he credits his Uncle Michael with planting the first seeds of sage advice when he opined that "the more he knew the less he knew." This soft nudge began his real education as a student of spirituality. Uncle Michael is now smiling from afar, for his pupil has finally graduated.

www.ingramcontent.com/pod-product-compliance
Lightning Source LLC
LaVergne TN
LVHW051633080426
835511LV00016B/2322